Man Eating Tiger of Bhim Bandh

By

James Corbett

Other animal stories by James Corbett

(1)Killer Snake

(2)Dog Eating Bears Of Sonepur

(3)Man Eating Tigers Of Chitwan

(4)Killer Elephant

Hindu to Christian conversion stories

(1)A Temple To Jesus Christ: Middle Class Incest

(2)A Temple To Jesus Christ: The Snake God

(3)A Temple To Jesus Christ: The Vultures Nest

Table of contents

Chapter(1) The Kill

The blue waters of the river looked beautiful and serene as it meandered through the lush green forests of Bhim Bandh forest reserve. Fish slapped their tails on the water top as ducks lazily swam around as they quacked at each other discussing something or the other. They weren't alone in the water. Accompanying them were a herd of deer called Sāmbar who relished nibbling at the water Hyacinth that grew on the banks. Accompanying them was a herd of Bara Singha's and Gaurs or water buffalo's. Some grunted as they chewed at the water hyacinth and lotus leaves that seemed to float on the water. Blue colored Kingfisher birds flew around in abandon occasionally stopping to hover like helicopters in mid air as they surveyed the water below them. They sometimes flew on or dived straight down into the water only to fly off with a small silver fish trapped in its beak. Lush green grass grew on the river banks on which wild boar, chital, sambar and water buffalo's grazed.

It was a Garden of Eden indeed. Or it wasn't. Unknown to the herbivores wallowing in the water, a tiger was hidden in the bushes twenty meters away. It was hunched on all fours with its body elongated as it kept a low profile hidden in the tall grass. It's ochre and black striped coat shone in the morning sun as it crouched hidden in the grass. It peered with unblinking eyes through the green blades at the delicacies in the water before it.

The tiger made some calculations. It would have loved to be in a position to attack which was within ten meters of the target. It had a heavy body and did not have the stamina to indulge in long distance chases. Like how the Cheetah or the leopard did. The tiger relied on surprise with an attack strategically launched from a close distance. Its safest bet to a kill was the surprise factor and a short chase. Everything was sudden. Even failure was swift. A short dash from the bushes, a short chase of an animal that had to start from zero speed and reach full speed in a fraction of a second while he himself was going full pelt at the target. If he missed, he wouldn't indulge in long tiresome chases which would sap his strength. He would simply stop, withdraw, and save his strength for a second attempt.

"Squawk."

The tiger peered up to see the source of the squawk. A crow was flying around in circles squawking its irritation at the tiger. The latter brought back his attention to the river as he peered through the grass to see if the squawks had attracted the deer's attention. Yes it had. The entire herbivore population in and around the lake had their ears pricked up and were looking towards the patch of high grass in which he was hidden.

The tiger twirled its tail as a peacock in the distance took up the crows warning. "Kwa-aa –kwa-aa," it called.

The tiger once more twirled its tail as the peacock sounded the alarm. The famous tiger alarm. Then silence for a minute.

"Kwa-aa-kwa-aa," the shrill alarm of the peacock broke the silence again. The deer that were grazing on the banks moved gingerly away from the tall grass. Chital deer looked sharply towards the tall grass as Bara Singha's raised their heads in surprise. The shrill alarm of the peacock broke the silence again. Another peacock picked up the call which was followed by the alarm call of a deer. Frenzied and frequent calling now surrounded the forest.

It was now or never.

The tiger braced itself and charged out of the tall grass and, like a cannonball out of a cannon, it charged across the open land towards the water's edge. It had targeted a deer that was sitting half immersed in water and was nibbling at lotus leaves.

There was total confusion in front of the river. Deer were darting in every direction, while the ones in the river beat the water into froth and spray as they thrashed through it in their desperation to get out of the river whose water hampered their speed. They desperately wanted to be on firm ground so that their hooves would get more traction.

Unmindful of the darting deer the tiger dashed straight into the river's edge, launched himself into the water and, thrashed powerfully through it in the direction of his prey. Sambar, chital, black buck, and water buffalo were fleeing in all directions forced by the tiger to go deeper into the river. Their movement was hampered by the weight of the water. The tiger crashed through the water amidst sheets of spray and swerved towards his chosen target to cut it off from the rest. His power and speed was amazing as he charged towards the Sambar which realized this and turned to its left. This caused the tiger to swerve to the left. The desperate deer thrashed the water and swerved to the right. The chasing tiger smashed through the water and swerved to the right. The desperate deer bucked and sliced through the spray as it tried to escape.

The tiger closed in fast pounding through the water with powerful strides. He was surprised at the speed and power he showed as he approached the deer. His paw smashed down on the huge creature with such force that both the hunter and the hunted disappeared into the water where the tiger grabbed the sambar's shoulder and turned his own head to grope for the throat. The underwater fight lasted for a minute. The tigers canines closed in a vice like grip around the neck which he snapped by jerking his head opposite to the deer's body. The tiger's feet touched the lake bed as the animal straightened its legs after which it appeared out of the water holding the deer's neck in its mouth. The latter kicked and thrashed the water in death throes while the other deer thrashed the water on their way to the banks of the lake from where they turned and watched. The sambar's thrashing soon died down so the tiger let go of the neck and took the tail into its mouth. He pulled the deer back to the river bank and dragged it towards the tall grass.

The deer that had reached the banks of the river stopped running and stood and looked at the tiger as it dragged its victim into the tall grass. The danger was over. The tiger had made its kill. One of them had died. Now they were safe for a couple of days till the tiger felt hungry again.

The tiger dragged the dead sambar through the tall grass till it reached a Peepal tree. It stopped and reclined on the ground panting heavily. It was tired. The sudden attack had sapped its strength. It was having a breather as it lay panting. After a five minute rest it proceeded to saw with its teeth and its strong jaws into the hide of the deer's rump. It made a gash in the rump, shoved its snout in and pulled out a chunk of flesh.

While the tiger chewed and chomped at the meet a celebration of a different kind was taking place two kilometers upstream in the jungle. It was the forest lodge of Bhim Bandh.

The lodge itself comprised of two British era cottages facing each other with a hot water swimming pool between the cottages. The swimming pool had steps that were six feet wide and led down into the water. There was a table on the pavement next to the swimming pool with chairs around it. Three teen aged boys and three girls sat at the table and were having a hearty meal of hot rice and spicy hot chicken curry. There were glasses on the table and a bottle of brandy. The six drank the alcohol as they ate their food.

It was a celebration. One of the teenagers, the tall one, was the son of a powerful politician who had just been appointed a minister in the Bihar Government. The other boys were his friends. The three had invited their girl friends to join them in the picnic. Now they had to be back home before sunset to join in the celebrations with their father. They had enjoyed driving and yelling and squealing around Bhim Bandh forest and were now enjoying their food.

"Hurry, finish your food," said the tall brat who sported chocolate brown skin and curly hair. "We have to go back."

The girls ate greedily as one of the boys took the jug of water and washed his hands in the plate. A bearer who worked for the forest department walked up to the table with a towel. He handed the towel to the boy who had just washed his hands.

"Sahib," the bearer said. He addressed the tall boy. "Sahib, your father has become a minister. Are there chances of him getting the charge of the ministry of forests?"

The tall teenager shook his head. "Don't know," he said. "It all depends on the chief minister."

"Sahib, can you help me. I would like to be transferred to a city. This forest life is boring."

"I'll think about it," said the tall boy. "I will help you in one condition. You are not to tell anyone that we brought these girls over."

"Sahib, I promise not to tell anyone."

The tall boy looked at the bearer. "Tell me; are there any tigers in this forest?"

The bearer smiled and nodded his head. "Yes there are two. They are T19 and T20."

The tall boy looked perplexed. "What's T19 and T20?"

"They are names the forest department has given the tigers that reside in this forest. The males name is Ashok and the females name is Machli."

"Why T19 and T20?"

"Sahib, T stands for tiger. And the number is given because the tigers are regularly counted. They are the nineteenth tiger and the twentieth tiger residing in the state of Bihar."

"Can I shoot one?"

"No sahib, they are a protected species. If anyone shoots a tiger, there is a big hue and cry over the killing. It becomes an international case. The international media gets involved and all hell breaks loose."

"I know that. But poaching does take place. I hear tiger skin is very expensive."

"Yes sahib, a tiger skin costs approximately thirty hundred thousand rupees."

The three friends and the girls finished eating. They washed their hands on the plates by taking jugs of water and pouring it on their hands washing them.

"Let's go," said a short stocky teen aged boy. His face was dotted by scars left by small pox. "We have to be back home before dark."

"What did you say the tigers names were?" the tall boy asked as he stood up.

"T20 and T19 sahib."

"These forest officers live a fairy tale life giving tiger's electronic codenames like T19 and T20."

The tallboy bent down and picked up a gun from the ground. It was an old British era single shot twelve gauge Stevenson with a single barrel and a brass cocking hammer. An ancient leather strap travelled from the barrel to the wooden butt. The weapons stock was ancient and showed gouges, scratches, the blood, sweat, and tears of decades of misuse. The barrel was pitted and rusted and was coated with several coats of black paint.

The tall boy picked up a blue bag that was lying on the ground. He opened the zipper and shoved his right hand in. The hand emerged from the bag holding three red colored cartridges for the gun. They were the famous LG cartridges and contained three deadly round balls each.

"Let's go," he said as he walked towards the Jeep. He handed the gun to a girl who was wearing a pair of blue jeans and a white top. "Here hold this gun and sit on the passenger seat next to me," he said as he shoved a cartridge into the breach into the mouth of the barrel.

The girl looked at the gun and felt uncomfortable at the thought of having to hold it. The tall boy recognized her hesitation. "Come on hold it," he goaded her. "Don't be afraid."

The girl reluctantly took the gun and held it awkwardly as she walked up to an old olive green world war II vintage Ford Jeep. It was an open Jeep with no hood with the collapsible windscreen lying on the bonnet. The tarpaulin hood had been folded neatly and was lying on the floorboard in the rear of the vehicle. The tall boy climbed into the driver's seat while the girl with the gun seated herself in the passenger seat next to him. The other boys and girls climbed into the rear of the vehicle and seated themselves.

The tall boy switched on the vehicles ignition causing the vehicles self starter to whine, the engine to cough, and finally roar to life. The boy pressed the clutch with his right foot, meshed the gears, let go of the clutch, and put his foot down on the accelerator. The Jeeps engine roared, and the vehicle trundled out of the guest house compound. Once out of the gates, the Jeep turned right and travelled along a rutted dirt track which ran through the jungle. The Jeep trundled on as it bucked and bounced over obstacles in the rutted road. The ancient leaf springs supporting the vehicles suspension winced from the beating the vehicle received from the uneven road.

The tall boy enjoyed the drive. He loved the vehicle, especially its rugged antique features. "Okay then, lets sing a song," he said.

The happily drunk group sang a Hindi song as the tall boy drove on parping the Jeeps horns to the tune of the song. The Jeep hit a little mud drain that ran across the road. It hopped out and hit the ground with a jarring thud causing the occupants hip girdles to take the shock. The vehicle approached a Jungle stream which crossed the road. The tall boy didn't slow down causing the Jeep to dash through the stream shooting up sheets of spray ten feet high. The happy occupants were soaked in water as the Jeep lurched and bounced and did a jig as it raced out of the stream. The tall boy had an excited grin on his face.

The jeep roared on and the occupants realized the road was meandering through the jungle. This wasn't reason for the tall boy to slow down. He was enjoying taking the bends at break neck speed. He maneuvered the vehicle around curves causing the tires to squeal with pain. The vehicle threw up dust as the body tilted to the right, then to the left and vice versa as the wheels spun and screamed as they negotiated each turn.

"Do you want to steer the vehicle?" the tall boy shouted to the gun holding girl above the roar of the vehicles ancient petrol engine.

The girl shook her head as the vehicle negotiated a curve. The tall boy suddenly braked causing the wheels to lock. The vehicle skidded over the gravel and stopped. The gun holding girl and the people sitting in the back were thrown forward. The gun holding girl braced herself and prevented herself from being thrown on to the bonnet by holding the vehicles dashboard while the people in the rear seats held on to their seats so as not to be thrown over the front seat occupants.

A tiger stood smack in the middle of the road fifty feet in front of the jeep. It was the tiger that had just killed the deer in the river. It had just had a hearty meal, hidden the carcass under some Magnolia bushes and had sauntered off. It was crossing the road to the other side when the Jeep had roared up and braked. The occupants looked at the magnificent creature as a chill ran down their spines. They felt vulnerable in the open Jeep. If the tiger attacked, they didn't have the protection the metal body of a car would have provided. The tiger simply had to charge, pounce into the Jeep and attack them.

The boys in the vehicle didn't know about the animal's recent kill and the fact that it had a full belly. It had been disturbed by the sudden appearance of the Jeep and the roar of the latter's ancient engine. That is why it had stopped its leisurely walk and turned to face the Jeep. The tiger was in no mood to kill anyone or anything now.

But the boys were city bred city slickers and did not know anything about tigers. They just knew it was a dangerous animal.

"Yeeeeeeeeeeeeeks," squealed the gun holding girl. She thought she was most vulnerable as she was sitting in the front seat and the rest were behind her. "It's a tiger. Help, help, help." She was on the verge of hopping out of the Jeep and running.

"My god, it's looking at us," squealed a boy who was sitting behind the gun holding girl. He had panicked and also was on the verge of hopping out of the Jeep and running down the road.

"It's going to pounce at us. Shoot it," the short stocky boy shouted. "Quick, you got a gun. Use it. Shoot it."

Still looking at the tiger, the tall boy held his right hand out to the girl sitting beside him and holding the ancient gun. His hand was trembling. "Give me the gun quick," he said. "It may attack."

The terrified girl handed the ancient Stevenson single shot gun, which was loaded, to the tall boy. She realized she had peed in her trouser in fright. The tall boy took the gun in his trembling hands and pulled back the brass hammer after which his thumb pushed the safety catch knob. The gun was cocked and ready to fire.

The tiger snarled at the Jeep. It was irritated with the roar of the Jeeps petrol engine.

"Shoot," said the short stocky boy. "Shoot before it attacks."

The tall boys trembling hands lifted the gun and placed the butte against his shoulder. He held the gun tightly and somehow aimed it at the snarling animals face. The tiger gave a low growl and sauntered forward.

"Shoot, damn it shoot," the short stocky boy yelled. "It is going to attack."

The tall boy aimed at the head and fired just as the tiger turned left to lope into the forest. There was a loud bang as the tall boy withstood the recoil. He felt the thud on his shoulder as the barrel swung to the left with the smoking end facing the terrified girl. The boy swung back swinging the barrel to once again face the tiger he had fired at. He didn't know that three deadly round red hot balls had smashed into the animals jaws blowing off its canine teeth and stunning it senseless. The tiger roared, sprang, and landed in the bushes where it lay shaking the bushes with its feet writhing in pain.

The Jeeps amazed occupants stared at the bush in which the tiger had landed. The bush rustled. Realization slowly seeped into them that the tiger had been hit.

"You got the tiger," the short stocky boy whispered in awe.

"Wow," the girl sitting in the front commented as she looked with awe at the bush.

"That was one hell of a shot. You killed the tiger with just one bullet," the third boy said. "Dou you realize what you have done. Man, you've shot a tiger."

It took the tall boy some time to soak in the fact that he had shot the tiger. He could not believe what he had just done. "Shit, I shot a tiger," he finally said.

"Man, you have just shot a tiger," the short stocky boy said. "The tiger is dead. You saved us."

"Let's dump the body into the Jeep and smuggle it out of the forest," the third boy suggested. He still found it hard to believe what had just happened. "Come on, don't be afraid. It's dead. Let's take it away before the forest officials come and confiscate it."

The Jeeps occupants climbed out of the vehicle.

"Be careful," said the tall boy as he pulled out the spent cartridge from the slot in the barrel. He dropped the spent shell on the ground and shoved a fresh one into the slot. "Be careful. It could still be alive."

"No, it's dead. I saw the bullet hitting the face," the short stocky boy said.

"I thought I saw the bullet hit its mouth," the third boy said as the group walked cautiously towards the bush in which the tiger lay.

"The mouth and face are the same thing," said the short stocky boy as the three walked cautiously towards the bush. "The mouth is situated in the face isn't it?"

The bush was in the right hand side of the road so the boys and girls crept up the left side edge of the road till they were just twenty feet away from the bush. They could see the ochre and white striped body as it lay on its side. The gun holding boy crept cautiously towards the tiger followed by the short stocky boy and the rest of the group. "Yes it is dead," said the tall boy as he lowered his guard and the gun. He walked two steps forward and realized his mistake.

The tiger wasn't dead. Half of its teeth had been blown off stunning it unconscious. It gained consciousness and saw the approaching humans. With one mighty roar, it sat up, and to the horror of the humans, sprang at them.

The tall boy panicked, dropped his gun, and ran while his friends screamed and ran behind him towards the Jeep. The stunned tiger loped into the Jungle. The picnickers reached the Jeep where the tall boy dived to the ground, rolled sideways, and found himself lying under the Jeeps chassis. The other boys did the same. It was everyone for himself. The screaming girls were the last to crawl under the chassis.

"The tiger will kill us," a girl squealed. "Help, help, help."

"Shut up and stop screaming," the tall boy scolded the girl as he pushed her out from under the vehicle with his feet. "Stop squealing or you will attract the tiger's attention to us."

The terrified girls were half outside and half under the Jeep. So they pushed and shoved at the boys, kicking with their legs, as they forced themselves deeper under the vehicle.

"Shut up, if you girls want to remain in here," the short stocky boy warned the girls.

The scared group lay under the Jeep thinking that the tiger would come and take one of them. But no tiger came. So they peered around. There was no tiger around.

"Where has the tiger gone?" the short stocky boy asked in a whisper.

"Idiot, stop whispering or you will attract its attention," the third boy whispered.

"Eeeeeeeeeeeeh,help,help,help," a girl squealed. "Help, it will kill us."

The tall boy cupped the girl's mouth with his palm. "Shut up," he whispered as the girls whimpered.

The terrified group stayed cooped under the Jeeps chassis for a whole ten minutes but no tiger came. So the tall boy got an idea. "I think it is waiting in some of those bushes on the side of the road. It is waiting for us to come out from under the Jeep," he said in a trembling voice. He was perspiring profusely.

"Now what are we to do?" the short stocky boy whispered. "How do we escape?"

The tall boy thought and thought and finally got an idea. "Let's make a rush for it. Let's rush out from here, climb into the Jeep and drive off. If the tiger attacks, it will get one of us, most probably one of the girls."

"What! Eeeeeeeeeeeeeh," a girl squealed. "Then why did you bring us here?" She started to cry.

Without signaling, the tall boy abruptly rolled out from under the vehicle, stood up, and hopped into the driver's seat. The other boys did the same. They rolled out from under the vehicle and climbed into the Jeeps rear. The tall boy switched on the vehicles ignition just as the girls crawled out and stood up.

"Come on, hurry and climb in. We are going," the short stocky boy shouted at the girls as he grabbed a girls hand and pulled her up. The other boy took his cue and pulled up a girl while the girl who had been holding the gun hopped into the passenger seat next to the tall driver as the vehicle roared off.

The tall boy meshed the gears, gunned the engine, and sped down the rutted dirt track unmindful of the hammering the ancient suspension was receiving from the rutted road. He wanted to be out of the forest and away from the tiger menace.

The Jeep sped on as its wheels kicked up dust. It soon reached the intersection where the rutted road entered the highway which ran through the forest. There was a pillion box to the right of the dirt track with two pillars on both sides of the track holding up an iron gate which was the entrance to the tiger reserve. The gate was shut and locked with a forest guard standing in front of the gate with a raised hand and open palm as a sign to the Jeep to stop. The vehicle braked and halted.

The forest guard walked over to the Jeep. "What happened?" he asked. "I heard a gunshot and a tiger's roar."

"Open the gate," the tall boy ordered.

"I heard a gunshot and a tiger's roar. It was T20's roar. Did you shoot the tiger?"

"No I didn't. Look in the Jeep. Do you see a gun in the Jeep? How can we shoot without a gun? Someone else must have done it."

"I will have to detain all of you," the guard said. "Till the matter is investigated."

"Mr," the tall boy said. "I don't think you know that my father has just been appointed a minister in the state cabinet. Open the gate, or I will be forced to get you thrown out of your job."

The forest guard looked at the boy. "You did wrong to shoot that tiger."

"I told you I didn't shoot it. I told you to check this vehicle for firearms. How can I shoot something without firearms? We don't have a gun. Neither did we see a dead tiger in the jungle."

"I will have to detain all of you," the guard repeated. He was stubborn.

The boys got down from the Jeep and opened the gate.

"You cannot do this. Don't use force on me. I have noted down your Jeeps number."

The boys walked back to the Jeep and climbed in. "I am going to the police station to report you to the police. We all saw your attempt to molest this girl," he said pointing to the girl who was sitting next to him. The girl shook her head in agreement.

The forest guard was scared. He knew these brats well. He realized that if he didn't let them go they would get him framed in a false attempt to rape case. He stared at the tallboy who switched on the Jeeps ignition.

The engine whined, coughed, and roared to life as the tall boy revved the engine to give it strength. He pressed the clutch pedal, meshed the gears, released the clutch pedal and sped off. The guard stared at the fast receding vehicle. "Brats," he said. "Low down brats."

The forest guard shut the gate.

Chapter(2) Failed hunt

It was a scene of peaceful calm serenity on both the banks of the river. An assortment of herbivores munched at the lush green grass that grew on the banks. Fishes in the river slapped their tails on the water top while birds flew around in abandon. As usual, there was an assortment of animals in the river nibbling at lotus leaves and the leaves of the water Hyacinth. And today a tiger sat crouched and hidden in the bushes as it peered through the blades of grass at the food he wanted to eat.

The tiger was T20, the tiger whose canines the tall brat's gun had blown off. He was now canine less and twenty days had passed since he had last killed a deer. Naturally, he was extremely hungry and desperately needed nourishment. It was vital for his health to somehow kill something today. He had attempted thrice at the animals in the river. But the animals he stalked and attacked, managed to fight him off and escape. His mouth pained, and it was impossible to get a proper grip on the hide of a deer or a wild boar without his canines. Yes, he had eaten. But that was a peacock and a peahen he had hunted and killed. But this was not enough to sustain his heavy body. He had to kill something big and fill his stomach. Only then would his mouth start healing. That is why T20 peered expectantly through the foliage.

He chose a sambar stag that was grazing a hundred feet away. He watched it as it grazed, looked up, looked around, munched its food and continued grazing. T20 made his calculations as the stag continued chomping at the grass. The wind was blowing from the stag to the tiger so the stag couldn't smell the stalker. Neither had the birds on the tree tops seen the tiger stealthily approach the bush in which it was hiding.

T20 suddenly burst out of the bushes and loped towards the sambar stag as the deer darted in different directions. The sambar stag that T20 had targeted darted towards the river. But it was too late. T20 was nearly on him. The desperate stag dashed into the water which only helped in slowing him down as his muddy hooves sank into the muddy river bed. T20 was on high ground so had the advantage of traction on hard ground to his favor. He pounded the ground with his paws as he approached the deer that was now thrashing the water into sheets of spray as it tried to escape.

At the last moment T20 leapt forward and landed on the grunting sambar's back. The tiger's weight and the underwater slush made it impossible for the sambar to gallop further into the water. It stood grunting as the tiger seemed to sit piggyback on its back.

T20 had trapped the sambar but did the mistake of getting off its back. His rear slid off the sambars back as he tried to dig his teeth into the hide. His feet touched the slushy river bed as his paws held on to both sides of the back. His teeth groped to get a hold on the hide.

The sambar realized the tiger's weight was not on his back. He turned around while T20 held on to his back. The sambar grunted and kicked back thrashing the water as he did so. T20 got kicked and was thrown two feet back but bounced back and grabbed the left rear thigh in his mouth. Though his mouth pained him, he held on as the sambar grunted and pranced around with its front feet thrashing the water. T20 held on. The sambar floundered allowing T20 to let go of the thigh and spring back onto the deer's back.

With the heavy tiger once more on its back, the sambar floundered with its fore legs giving way sending the hunter and the hunted plunging into the water. The stricken sambar heaved up as it thrashed the water causing the tiger to once more spring at its rump. It stood on its hind legs and grabbed the rump in its paws.

The sambar pranced around to shake off the tiger but T20 held on. His hind feet were firmly on the ground while his chest was on the struggling sambar's rump. The tiger put its right forepaw over the back and gripped it trying to use his weight to pull the sambar down. It tried to bite the throat but missed and snapped its mouth shut.

The sambar fought back by using its strength to remain standing as the tiger tried to pull it down. It was unsuccessful, so it engulfed the lower hide of the sambars throat in its mouth to get some sort of grip on the throat.

The stag jerked away and T20 was thrown off. He reacted with lightning speed and went for the neck. The sambar realized the tiger would go for his throat so he swiveled around. With the neck out of reach, T20 attacked the belly and the hind legs and once more got a grip on the right rear thigh forcing the deer to sit down in twelve inches of water. For a second the two sat as though they were frozen.

The sambar suddenly kicked its legs and shook T20 off, got up, and ran out of the water. T20 sprang at the deer and loped after it. The sambar was out of the water and was on hard ground so it got the traction it needed to run with speed. T20 loped after it, sprang, and grabbed its tail. His forepaws slammed into the ground to stop his own running and slow down the deer to finally stop. This resulted in the herbivores, who were watching the fight from a distance, witnessing the ridiculous sight of a loudly grunting sambar stag drag a tiger, with its tail in the latter's mouth, across the moss and lichen covered ground of the river bank. T20's teeth clenched hard at the tail refusing to let it go. The tail did not take the tigers load and snapped. T20 was thrown sideways with the tail still in his mouth while the free but tailless sambar galloped off downstream along the river bank. With a burst of adrenaline it dashed into the undergrowth and disappeared leaving a panting T20 with one more failed attempt at killing a deer to his credit.

The tiger made one last attempt to chase the deer. He loped after it and charged into the undergrowth. But he soon got tired so he stopped and watched the sambar disappear into the jungle.

T20 was panting heavily so he reclined on the grassy ground. It was necessary for him to kill something and eat. He was extremely hungry. He had lost most of his strength in the fight with the deer. This was his fourth attempt to kill a deer and the fourth time he failed. He had successfully stalked his target, came close to it, chased it, pounced on it, and captured it. But his teeth and the tormenting pain in his mouth did not allow him to kill the victim.

The tiger lay back and snapped at some flies that buzzed around him. It was amply proved that his mouth had failed him. It would not allow him to capture and kill a prey. The only food option left to him was the humans in the human villages in the area. He would have a go at them. That's if he wanted to eat.

Chapter(3) Human kill.

It was a bright sunny morning and a group of women sat on a three foot broad cemented pavement that traveled around the well. They used a rope and a bucket to pull out buckets of water to do their washing. They chatted with each other and washed their clothes while some of them took turns to drop the bucket into the well and pull out a bucketful of water. Their husbands had gone into the jungle to fetch firewood.

It was the village of Rampur. It was situated on the edge of the Bhim Bandh forest. To the right was the forest while to the left was around three hundred acres of verdant fields. Wheat fields which belonged to the village. The villagers were all petty farmers whose ancestors had cleared the forest and settled there. The villagers knew about T19 and T20. What they didn't know was T20 had become rogue and was at the moment silently stalking the village and coming towards it for food.

The tiger crouched low and crawled forward concealing himself behind ferns and some magnolia bushes. It peered at the women washing clothes around the well. It was hungry and wanted food. It had failed to kill the sambar stag. The humans seemed to be an easy target.

The tiger cocked his ears as he heard sounds behind him. They were human sounds. It sniffed the air. Yes, it was the smell of humans. They were coming from somewhere behind him.

The tiger stealthily turned around in the bush. He was now facing the area which he thought the approaching humans would walk down. He crouched low and waited.

Sure enough, a group of fifty male villagers walked into the tigers view. They were carrying bundles of wood on their heads which they had collected in the jungle. They chatted with each other as they walked on oblivious of the danger hidden in the bushes waiting for them.

The humans continued walking and neared the bushes. Without giving a warning the tiger roared and sprang at them. Unfortunately for it, the wood cutter it had targeted and pounced at, was faster than what he thought. The man saw the tiger burst out of the greenery and spring at him. He reacted by throwing the pile of wood at the springing tiger. The wood hit the tiger's snout while the latter was in mid flight causing it to see stars. The tiger roared as it brushed the bundle of wood aside, landing on the ground missing his target.

"Tiger," a wood cutter shouted as he threw his bundle and ran. The other humans threw their bundles and ran through the jungle foliage as fast as they could. By the time the tiger recovered and stopped seeing stars, the humans were out of the forest and running down the village's single street.

"Tiger, tiger, run, hide indoors," the villagers yelled as they ran towards their mud huts.

"Aiieeeeee," the women who were sitting around the well screamed as they dropped what they were carrying or left what they were doing and ran towards their mud huts. "Help, help, help," they screamed. They had heard the tiger's wild roar and the men folks yells. Within minutes the single street in the village was empty. Everyone had disappeared indoors.

T20 walked to the edge of the forest and looked down the village's single street. It growled a challenge to the villagers and walked down the street taking in the different smells that emanated from the huts. It peered to the right and peered to the left and peered into a couple of mud paved alleys. But there was no human outside. Everyone was indoors with the doors locked and sealed. The street was empty. Not even a goat or a chicken roamed the street.

The tiger walked up the single street to the end of the village. It turned around and walked down the path it had just come. People peered through slits in doors and windows at the passing tiger.

"The tiger has become bold," whispered a villager who was peering at the road through a crack in his cheap wooden door.

"It will eat us," the wife squealed. She was hiding under a bed.

"Stop squealing," the husband scolded the woman. "Your squealing will attract its attention to this house. It seems like it wondered out of the forest into our village by mistake."

The tiger boldly sauntered through the single street and stopped. It heard a faint sputtering noise so it turned to its right and peered into an alley between two mud shacks. It saw a tractor sputtering across a field in the distance. It was a red colored International Mc Cormick tractor which had turned right and was sputtering across the fields towards the village. The tiger quietly sat down and waited as the tractor bucked and bounced over the uneven ground towards the village. It waited patiently as the tractor approached the last hut. The vehicle inexplicably turned right towards the entrance to the village's single street. It was driven by a bare backed turbaned driver.

The tiger waited in the alley as the driver steered the loudly sputtering vehicle into the single street. The driver was surprised to see the street empty. Not even a stray dog roamed around. There wasn't even a cow or a chicken in sight. They were also inhabitants of the village. The tractor driver shrugged and drove on. "Where had everyone and every living soul gone?" he wondered. "And why?"

The tractor sputtered on as the driver looked around at the empty street. His thatched hut was just two hundred feet down the road.

The tiger waited as the noisy tractor approached the spot near where he was sitting. The tractor sputtered into view. T20 yawned, stood up, crouched, twirled his tail and let out a low growl.

The tractor driver heard the growl. It came from behind him so he turned around in time to see the tiger charge at him. Unlike other motor vehicles, a tractors accelerator is a simple rod protruding from under the steering wheel. The panicked driver slammed the rod down to full throttle causing the tractor to emanate a roar as it spewed out thick black smoke from its exhaust as it spurted forward just as the tiger sprang. Naturally, the tiger miscalculated as the tractor had spurted forward and was out of the tigers reach. The tiger missed the vehicle and landed on the ground behind the escaping tractor. It immediately gathered itself and loped after the tractor and soon caught up. Unfortunately for the driver, the maximum speed of the tractor was forty miles an hour. And the vehicle was old. It was impossible for it to outrun the loping tractor. The tiger made another attempt to spring onto the vehicle. It roared and sprang and landed on the left rear mud guard next to the driver. The terrified driver swung his left leg over the vehicles gears and steering wheel and hopped off the running tractor. Driverless, the tractor swerved to the right, hit a mud wall, and straightened itself. It sputtered straight into a fifteen feet high hay stack. The tiger roared as it was forced into the haystack. It roared a second time and hopped off the stricken vehicle which was digging itself deeper into the haystack. The tiger turned and loped after the running screaming driver. The tractor went right through the haystack, came out of the other side half covered with hay, hit a mud wall, and turned over on its side on the field behind the haystack with the engine roaring its plight to the world and the rear wheels spinning uncontrollably.

The driver continued screaming as he ran. "Help," he yelled to his wife. "Quick open the door, a tiger is chasing me."

The tiger sprang landing squarely on the drivers back knocking the turban off causing the driver to plunge to the ground. The tiger adjusted itself as it snarled and realized it had the man straddled under him. The man turned over on his back and screamed. He braced his legs against the ground and pushed hard pushing his body out from under the tiger.

A door of a hut to the right of the stricken man opened and a screaming woman ran out holding an eight foot long bamboo pole just as the tigers paw slapped her husband's face silencing his screams. The horrified woman saw her husband being silenced as the tiger caught her husband's neck in his jaws. "Aiieeeeee," she screamed as she ran forward swinging the pole down on the tiger hitting T20 squarely on the head. This brought a roar from T20 as he sprang for the woman only to receive a second shot from the pole. The woman screamed, dropped the bamboo pole, turned around, and scampered back into her hut.

"Help," the woman yelled from inside the hut. "Help, the tiger is killing my husband." The woman peered through a crack in her door and saw the tiger take hold of the unconscious mans neck in his jaws. It lifted the neck and dragged the unconscious figure on his way out of the village to the privacy of the forest.

The woman was desperate so she opened her door and peered out at the tiger dragging her husband away. "Help, it has killed my husband," the woman yelled. "Help, help, help, it is dragging my husband away."

The appeal fell on deaf ears as people cautiously opened windows and peered out. Some of them saw the tiger drag the man's body to the village exit. They quietly watched as none of them had the courage to challenge the tiger and recover the stricken man's body.

"Help, please anyone has a gun?" the woman screamed the question. "Please kill the tiger before it kills my husband. Help, help, help."

Nobody dared leave their hut. They quietly watched as the tiger dragged the body out of the village into the jungle. The woman was desperate. So she opened her door and ran to the spot where the tiger had attacked her husband. The tiger had disappeared into the forest with the body so the bereaved woman fell sobbing to the floor. Doors and windows finally opened and people stepped out of their homes. But no one dared to go near the women. They were ashamed of themselves.

T20 had executed his first human kill. It was now a dangerous man eater.

Chapter(4) A retired American hunter

The forest officer was a tall man with a fair complexion. He was sitting in a railway coach with several other passengers on his way to the remote rural railway station of PUSA. From there he would take a Tonga and travel on the famous PUSA road to the remote little town of PUSA.

PUSA is well known all over north India as an Agricultural University run by the Indian Government. Very few people know what its actual name meant. PUSA actually stood for Phibb's USA. Two American brothers namely William Phibb's and Jonathan Phibb's migrated to India from California way back in the 1890's to start a stud farm to supply the British Colonial Government of India with well bred horses. Those were the days when the horseless carriage was just making an appearance in British and American newspapers. Travel was still done on horseback and stud farm owners were making a killing. Naturally, there was competition between the stud farms, and owners were in constant lookout for greener pastures. India with its road less landmass, an abundance of deposed and rich kings and queens, a rich landed aristocracy nurtured by the British, and a Caucasian Government in full control, was the greenest pasture. India was a carrot beckoning the Phibb's family to come over. It had become a sort of El Dorado, a land of gold for stud farmers. Seventy percent of Britain's male population were employed in India and were leading princely lives. And the only mode for short distance travel was horse back or the slow bullock cart. Horse drawn carriages were in huge demand as they were six times faster and more comfortable than the slow moving bullock cart. So well bred horses were in high demand.

William Phibb's and Jonathan Phibb's crossed over with their families and bought a three thousand acre farm near the village of Ramnagar. The stud farm was named Phibb's USA, in short PUSA. This was done so that people knew it was an American enterprise. The village of Ramnagar and the remote railway station were renamed PUSA. And the road leading from the stud farm to PUSA became the famous PUSA road of today.

The Phibb's family enjoyed life in India. It was a royal life complete with a private hospital for the farms employees and a separate colony for the trainers and jockeys. It even had its own captive thermal power plant for electricity. In fact PUSA stud farm was the only place in northeastern India that boasted of a luxury called electricity in the early 1900's. But unfortunately good things don't last long. The disastrous earthquake of 1936 shook the entire Phibb's farm causing the luxurious mansion that Phibb's had constructed to collapse on the entire Phibb's family killing everyone except for Jonathan Phibb's and Williams son Jeffrey. Jonathan was a broken man. He now hated the country and wanted to go back home. He sold the entire property to the British colonial Government of India and returned to the US a broken man. Jeffrey stayed back and took up a local native woman for a wife. After Indian independence, he applied for an Indian citizenship and got it. His son Henry Phibb's competed in the Indian Administrative service examinations and bagged a high ranking job in the Indian forest department. That was after he married an Anglo Indian girl. Henry was retired now and lived in PUSA near the ruins of the mansion which had collapsed on his ancestors. He received his government pension which was negligible. Most of his income came from his forty acre fish farm and five acre poultry farm. In short, he was well to do by Indian standards.

Henry Phibb's had been a class one hunter of his time. His house, a two storied structure was the proud owner of stuffed animals that he had shot during his years as a forest officer. It was to meet him and to request him to come and help the forest department capture or kill T20 that the forest officer was travelling to PUSA in the train today.

The forest officer's name was Ram Singh. He was tall, wore a white half sleeved shirt and grey trousers. He looked out of the window at the passing country side and realized the train was approaching a station.

"What is the name of this station," the forest officer asked his fellow passengers.

"PUSA,"the dhoti clad passenger replied.

The train whistled as it stopped chugging and slowed down. Steam spewed out of the engine in loud hisses as the engine wheezed. The coach the forest officer was sitting in was filled with the acrid stench of burning grease as the brakes locked the wheels.

"How far is it to PUSA agricultural farm?" the forest officer asked.

"Forty kilometers," was the reply. "Who do you want to meet there?"

"He is an American," the forest officer said.

"Are you going to meet Henry sahib?"

"Yes, I am to meet Henry sahib," the forest officer said as he smiled. "Do you know where he lives?"

"Everyone in this area knows Henry sahib and his fish farm. He is a popular man and a good man."

The train's wheels squealed in jarring metallic sounds as the train stopped. The forest officer got up to leave and on second thoughts turned to face the man he was speaking to. Can you tell me how I can reach his place?"

"No problem,' the passenger replied. "Walk out of the railway station compound and you will see a line of horse driven carts called Tonga's. All the Tonga drivers know where Henry sahib lives. They will take you to him."

The forest officer thanked the man and walked to the exit gate of the coach. He stepped out onto the stations platform and looked around. It was a small station with the station building positioned strategically in the middle of the platform. The building was actually a small three roomed structure which housed the ticket office, the station masters office which doubled as a lounge and the station entrance, and the luggage office. Half of the platform was covered by a tin shed under which he was standing.

The forest officer entered the lounge and walked out of the station. He walked down three steps and stood on a cemented enclosure which was the railway stations car park, or to be more precise, the stations horse cart park. There were twelve two wheeled carriages parked in a row in front of the station building. They were each driven by a single horse and were called Tonga's. The forest officer walked towards the Tonga's and realized that a dozen Tonga drivers had surrounded him.

"Sahib, where do you want to go?" they all asked in unison. It seemed as though they would either snatch or grab the single passenger that had left the station.

"I want to go to PUSA."

"Where to in PUSA?"

"To Henry sahib's house. Do you know him?"

The Tonga drivers squabbled amongst themselves for the lone passenger. This irritated the forest officer so he walked through them, walked past them, to a red colored Tonga which was pulled by a white horse. He climbed onto the Tonga and sat down on the passenger seat. The Tonga drivers realized the lone passenger had settled the dispute by choosing the Tonga he wanted to ride in so they stopped quarrelling. A dhoti clad elderly bearded man walked out of the group to the Tonga. He was the vehicles owner and the driver. "Where would you like to go?" he asked.

"To PUSA, to Henry sahibs fish farm."

"It will cost you fifty rupee's."

The forest officer nodded his head so the Tonga driver picked up a whip from the vehicles floorboard, took the horses reins, sat on the seat next to the forest officer, jerked the reins, and whipped the horse's rump with the whip. The whip was super effective and with a jolt the Tonga lurched forward.

The horse clip clopped onto the tarmac pulling the Tonga along the famous PUSA road. After an hour and a half of clip clopping down the road, the Tonga entered a little village. It was the village of PUSA. The horse clip clopped down the single street. Seeing the village surroundings, the forest officer realized that the village was well of, and not like most north Indian villages. There weren't any mud houses and most of the plots boasted of a motorcycle standing proudly in front of a cottage.

The horse clopped on and passed by the entrance of the Indian Agricultural University. It clopped past the ancient deserted thermal power plant which lit up the entire stud farm more than a hundred years ago. The Tonga continued in its leisurely pace and passed the Phibb's brothers private hospital which was now the property of the Government of India and was a government hospital.

"There is Henry sahib's house," the Tonga driver said as he pointed to a cottage nestled cozily in a mango grove behind two fish ponds. The water area of each of the ponds was four hundred thousand square feet with a graveled road travelling between the two ponds to an open plot of land in front of the British era cottage.

"Take me to the cottage," the forest officer ordered the Tonga driver.

The Tonga driver obeyed and whipped the horse causing it to pick up speed. The Tonga trundled down the private road that travelled between the ponds. It approached the cottage in front of which there was a garden umbrella stuck to the ground. There was a table surrounded by four chairs under the garden umbrella. An elderly Caucasian couple sat under the umbrella listening to a radio and sipping beer. The male had a cheroot in his mouth.

"That old man smoking the cheroot is Henry sahib," the Tonga driver said. "And that woman is his wife. Her name is Elizabeth memsahib."

The Tonga driver hopped off the vehicle and bent down low in a reverent Namaste to the elderly American and his wife. "Namaste Henry sahib and Namaste Elizabeth memsahib," he said.

The elderly couple acknowledged the greeting with a nod of their heads. The elderly man peered at the approaching forest officer and smiled when he recognized him. He stood up to welcome him. "Hello Ram Singh," he said. "What a pleasant surprise to see you here."

The forest officer smiled as he took Henry's hand in his own and shook it. The two had been posted in Dehra Dun together where Henry Phibb's was Ram Singhs senior officer. That was before he retired. Now Ram Singh was a high ranking forest officer himself.

"Hello sir," Ram Singh wished back. "Long time no see sir."

"Yes we are meeting after a long time," Henry replied. "Well I am leading a retired life now."

The forest officer turned and took Elizabeth Phibb's outstretched hand in his own and shook it. "Hello Liz madam," he wished her.

"Come Ram Singh sit down," Henry said as he offered the forest officer a chair. "What brings you here?"

Ram Singh and the American couple seated themselves. Henry crossed one leg over the other and still puffing at his cheroot he proceeded to listen.

"Henry sir, the Government of India, to be more precise, the forest department officers in New Delhi sent me to give you an offer."

"Now Ram Singh, don't tell me that they want me to join the service again. The pay is miserable."

"Sir, the forest department has no intention of re employing you. They are offering you prize money. Do you remember T20. He was your baby. You nurtured him and watched him grow up. He was your baby."

"Yes, I remember T20. The tiger of Bhim Bandh tiger reserve. Actually I remember there were two of them. T19 and T20."

"Yes sir. The bad news is that T20 has gone rogue. It has become a man eater."

"But it was a disciplined tiger. It was used to seeing humans on Jeeps wanting to spot it."

"Sir, unfortunately it has become a man eater."

Henry turned to his wife. "Liz, could you please bring Ram Singh something to eat. He must be hungry. It is a long and tiring journey in outdated trains from Bhim Bandh to PUSA."

Elizabeth Phibb's got up and walked to the cottage. She disappeared indoors. "Elizabeth madam has got lovely golden hair," Ram Singh commented.

"It's not golden. The proper word for it is blond," Henry said.

"Henry sahib, is this the land that your ancestors bought and developed?" The forest officer asked. "I have heard the legend."

"It's not a legend because it really happened," Henry replied. "This whole area was developed by Jonathan and William Phibb's. They were my ancestors."

"The legend is that they had a very big house. It was magnificent. Where is it?"

Henry pointed to the east. There was a huge mud mound with some ruins on it. "That was my ancestral home. That was before the earthquake of 1936 destroyed it and killed my ancestors," Henry explained. "Now come to the point. Why are you here? You were talking of money before you changed the topic."

"Sir, T20 has become a nuisance. It has killed forty people in the villages in and around Bhim Bandh forest. The authorities want you to capture it or kill it. If possible capture it."

"But I am retired. I may lead a busy life here handling my affairs, but I lead a relaxed life."

"Sir, all of us officers in the forest department request you to accept the Governments offer. Many of us would like to see you back with us, even if it is only for a short period of time. You were a very popular officer."

"Ram Singh, you know as well as me that it takes time and patience to track and capture a tiger. It's easier to shoot it. I've grown old and do not have the time and patience to go tracking in mosquito infested jungles. My hunting days are behind me. Why don't you invite someone else?"

"That is the problem. Whom do we invite to track and hunt the tiger and maybe capture it? Times have changed. These are times of forest conservation. Not hunting. We are trained to protect the forests, not to hunt in it. There are trackers in the forest department but no hunters. Who hunts nowadays? Hunters are not needed. Their type has gone extinct except for a few old ones left alive. Sir, forgive me for saying this. You happen to be one of them."

Henry Phibb's thought for a moment. His right shoe scraped the ground as he spoke. "And what will they pay me. I will not accept the measly pay they pay forest officers. I will have to leave this place for a month or so. I will have to eat. And there are other expenses."

"The forest department will give you fifty thousand a month for your work. If you manage to capture T20 you will be rewarded with three hundred thousand rupees as prize money. And if you simply kill it the reward will be less. It will be one hundred thousand rupees. That is two hundred thousand less than what you would get if you captured it alive."

"You mean one hundred thousand rupees for a kill?"

"Yes sir, one hundred thousand rupees if you kill it. But the forest department will appreciate it if you capture it alive."

Henry looked askance at the pond where a fish had slapped the water with its tail creating ripples which seemed to swim away making round circles in the water. A blue colored kingfisher hovered over the water targeting a fish. "Now look at that thief," Henry said. "He's going to steal my fish from right under my nose."

Sure enough, the kingfisher fell beak downwards like a stricken fighter plane, straight into the water. It emerged and flapped its wings as it flew off with a silver fish writhing trapped in its beak.

"That was a silver carp the bird stole," Henry said laughing. He turned and looked at Ram Singh. "And what other perks do I get?"

"Sir, you will have your own cook and servants. Food items will be provided by the forest department for free. You will reside in a guest house of your choice. Ammunition that you need will be supplied to you. You will get a Jeep and a driver. And I will accompany you as your helper."

"Good, I agree. When do I come?"

"When ever it is convenient for you. But come soon before another human is killed."

"Okay, I will come day after tomorrow."

Chapter(5) Midnight killer

The village of Barhi was situated on the northern tip of the Bhim Bandh forest. It could be said that the village was nestled within the forest periphery itself. The inhabitants were marginal farmers who eked out a living by growing wheat and paddy in the little patches of land they had cleared from the forest. There was a nearby dam which blocked the outlet of a stream creating a nice little lake with hills on three sides and a dam on one. The dam supplied water to the villagers to irrigate their fields.

The dwellings in the village were mud huts as the people were poor and could not afford proper brick and concrete structures. The thatched roofs were made of material that was available for free in the forest. None of the huts had tables or chairs or cots which are regarded as basic furniture by civilized society. Neither did the huts have toilets or bathrooms. The villagers were in a habit of defecating in and around the adjoining fields or in the forest. The women washed their dirty linen in the nearby jungle stream that flowed from the dam.

The dam itself was a source of free food. Fish was available and could be easily caught. That is why a group of bare backed villagers had climbed down the Dams embankment and were sitting on the banks at the water's edge holding crude fishing rods made of five foot long sticks with a thread hanging from the stick. A hook was tied to the thread and was submerged under water with a dead earth worm hooked to the hook. Each man had a little basket made of dried reeds lying on the ground next to him. The baskets contained fish the people had caught.

Sitting on the banks of the lake, it became evening. So the group packed up and packed their little baskets containing the fish they had caught. They tied the baskets in bundles of cloth, climbed up the dam's embankment, crossed over to the other side, and climbed down the embankment to a path that led away.

While the people walked back to their village, they picked up dry wood or dry sticks they found littered on the path, resulting in them collecting a neat little pile under their arms as they reached the village. As usual, it was an impoverished village with a single street, which was actually an alley, which travelled through the village into the forest beyond.

The group of men entered the alley and dispersed as they reached their homes. The headman's house was the last hut in the row on the edge of the forest.

The village headman was a strong man. He was well built, around five feet eleven inches tall, with a bald head which was hidden from the world with a turban. He was the village headman, that's why his co villagers called him Mukhiyaji.

The headman walked to his hut whose door was open. He peered in. Sure enough, his wife was sitting in a corner of the hut and cooking some chapatti's on a fire over a mud stove. The room was stuffy as it was filled with bluish smoke. The village headman was used to this. In fact most of the villagers were used to the blue smoke of cooking fires. It was part of their everyday life.

The headman walked into the hut and dropped the pile of wood he had collected on the floor. His wife was sitting cross legged on the mud floor of the house next to the mud stove. "Here take the wood and take this basket of fish," he said as he handed the little basket that held eight little fishes he had caught in the lake. He looked around the one roomed hut and realized his son wasn't there. "Where is our son?" he asked.

"He's playing with the other kids of the village."

"Foolish woman. Didn't I tell you that a dangerous tiger is roaming in this area? It has become a man eater. Everyone should be in the village and in his home by night fall. Why are the kids playing outside in the dark?"

"I told him not to go out, but he disobeyed me and ran out."

"Foolish woman, go and fetch him. I will give him a spanking and you are not to protect him from me."

The headman moved to walk out but was stopped by his wife. "If we aren't allowed to go out after dark, then how are we supposed to defecate? We villagers don't have any toilets and the only place to defecate in is in the jungle. Since ancient times, men folk defecate in the jungle during daytime and women do it in the darkness of the night. Darkness gives us women the privacy we need. If we defecate during the day, the men folk will hide in the forest or creep up to the spot we are defecating in and peep at our bottoms. And maybe rape us."

The headman looked at his wife. This was a genuine problem. The villagers and he were too poor to afford latrines, let alone bathrooms. The men defecated in the forest during the day and no one peeped on them. It wasn't a prestige issue. But it was a prestige issue if people spied and saw a bathing wife's naked body or a defecating wife's naked bum. That is why it was an unwritten rule in all the villages in and around the forest of Bhim Bandh. Women defecated in the forest in the privacy of the night. Before dawn took over the firmament, they would have their bath and collect water from the nearby stream and bring it back to the village. Men folk defecated and bathed after dawn. If they entered the forest after dark then most probably they were peeping toms who would be one day punished.

"This is a genuine problem," the headman said. "To hide your vanity, you women will have to risk the tiger during the night. We cannot allow you to defecate during the daytime. You women are our prestige."

The headman walked out of the hut and stopped outside. He peered back in. "Three respectable male elders will escort the women folk tonight when they go to defecate. "The women will need protection in case the tiger attacks."

The headman walked away. He reached the village square and sat down under a Peepal tree with some villagers. They had a little chat and the headman made his point. "How will the women go to defecate in the forest today?" he asked. "The forest department people warned us that the tiger has been seen nearby."

"The women will have to defecate during the night," stated a short bare backed villager. "They cannot defecate during daytime. I will not allow that. Tiger or no tiger, they will defecate only in the night. I don't want rascals of my village and those of nearby villages to peep at my wife's' bottom while she is defecating."

The headman nodded his head in agreement. "Three responsible elders will accompany the women," he said. "It will be their job to bring the women back safely. They will be armed with spears to ward off wild animals and peeping toms."

A group of children ran into view. A naked boy led them. He was the head man's son. So the headman called out to the boy. "Arun, let's go home. Your mother is waiting for you with your dinner. She has cooked fish today."

The chocolate brown skinned boy ran up to his father and took hold of the latter's extended hand. He had a running nose which caused him to sniff at intervals. Together, the father and son walked to their hut. They entered it and realized that there were two plates ready with five chapatti's each and fish curry. The child would eat in the same plate as his mother.

The village headman sat cross legged behind his plate and proceeded to eat. His wife did the same. The three tore into the chapatti's, stuffed them with half a fish and stuffed the food into their mouths. They drank up the gravy. Nothing was to be wasted.

The headman burped and looked at his wife. "Three people will escort you all to the defecating spot," he said. "I will be one of them. We males will look the other way while the females defecate."

The wife was wearing a torn faded red sari and had cheap metal trinkets hanging from her ear lobes and nose. She giggled. "It's not necessary to look the other way," she said. "It will be too dark to see anything at all."

The headman smiled and continued eating. He soon finished his meal. So he got up, picked up a wooden jug from a corner of the room, dusted his bottom, went to the mud pot containing water, took a jug full of water, walked out of the room and washed his hands. He re entered the hut and sat cross legged on the bed of straw on which he and his wife usually slept.

The wife finished eating, washed her hand outside the shack and came back in. I think we should go and get the other women who want to defecate. It's getting late. We will do the needful and come back as early as possible."

The headman agreed, picked up a torch and a seven foot long iron spear from the ground. The two walked out of the hut. They turned and walked down the alley with the wife calling out to her friends. "Whoever wants to attend natures call, come and join us," she yelled peering into the doorway of each hut as they passed.

Women walked out and joined the couple. They all had ancient wooden jugs which their men folk had carved out of stumps of trees or from thick branches. The jugs were filled with water. Three more male villagers accompanied the little group. They shone their torches down the path that they had taken and were soon out of the village and in the jungle. They walked on listening to the night sounds which seemed so peaceful. The village headman and the other men knew this part of the jungle well. They lived here. They led the group of twittering women to an open patch of land.

"I think this is a good enough spot for you all to defecate in," the headman said. "We shouldn't go too far into the jungle."

The women walked to the patch of open land and looked at the men as a sign to switch off their torches. The men obeyed and switched off the flashlights allowing the area to be plunged into darkness. The women felt comfortable in the dark. They put their wooden jugs down on the ground, pulled up their sari's to their hips, sat down on their haunches and were soon sputtering and farting out the muck that was inside them.

The men didn't mind the noise. It was part of nature. Neither did the tiger mind the noise. It liked the noise as it was hungry and the noise attracted him and helped him home in on the women in the dark. He had been lurking in the foliage stalking the village and eyeing his prey when he saw the group of women walk into the forest. It silently, stealthily, and noiselessly trailed them out of the village. It was hiding in the bushes listening to the sputters and the farts. In the dark, the sputtering and the farts helped him zero onto a target. He zeroed onto the head man's wife. She was farting the most.

The lady was defecating and chatting with her friends when she felt something heavy push her back. Confused, she fell back on her own shit and realized the heavy thing had straddled her. She groped with her hands to make out what was on top of her. Her groping hands felt the tigers face who in turn was groping for her face. The woman failed to realize it was a tiger though she felt the furry body.

"Who are you?" the woman asked. "What are you doing on top of me?"

The woman heard a low growl right on her face. Her husband and the other men heard the growl. The husband switched on the flashlight and swung the beam around to focus it on the defecating women. He was embarrassed to see the woman's bare defecating bottoms. The flashlight beam swung around the open patch of land and stopped when the light hit the tiger. It was right in the middle of the group of defecators and was straddling his wife.

The wife saw the tiger in the glare of the light which for a second confused the animal into inaction. "Aiieeeeeee," the woman screamed as the flashlight blinded the tiger confusing it.

The other defecators were horrified to see the tiger right in their midst. It was T20. He had been attracted by the headman's wife's sputtering and farts which caused him to target her and lead him to her.

"Aiieeee," the woman screamed as she kicked up.

The tiger roared and was on the verge of snapping his mouth shut on the woman's face when a spear hit his mouth. It was the headman's spear. The latter's reflex was fast. Without thinking, as soon as he switched on the flashlight and saw the tiger straddling his wife, he swung his spear holding hand at the tiger sending the spear flying through the foliage at the tiger. It hit the tigers face stunning it but did not pierce the skin or break a bone. The spear head was old, rusted, and blunt. The tiger reacted by springing at the flashlight. The flashlight flew out of the headman's hand as he was thrown back on the ground. The flashlight fell three feet away and its light beam shone in the opposite direction on the tiger. The headman was in the dark while the tiger was caught in the flashlights glare. This confused the tiger. It crouched and with an ear splitting roar it sprang towards the spot it thought the headman would be. But there was no headman. The latter had rolled to the left and retrieved his spear. "Run," he yelled to his wife as he lifted the spear above his head to spear the tiger. "Run for your life. Don't worry about me."

The wife was now free as the confused tiger had sprung away. She saw the torch and crawled towards it. Her body had frozen with fright. She panicked and lunged for the torch and instead of grabbing it she missed and hit the end with her outstretched palm. The flashlight swiveled around with the beam focusing on the headman. The tiger was now in the dark. It could see the humans while the humans couldn't see him. It roared and sprang at the headman while the wife grabbed the torch, got up and ran. The forest was once more plunged into darkness.

The headman heard the tigers roar as it sprang at him. He rolled sideways just as the tiger landed on the spot where he had been. The wife was running away with the flashlight for all she was worth smacking through the leaves and ferns as she ran. Darkness once more confused the tiger as it roared and swiveled around. To his right he could hear the headman crash through the undergrowth in the dark. The latter was running for all he was worth mindless of the battering his face and body were receiving from the undergrowth.

The woman ran towards the entrance of the village. The tiger chose her and decided to chase her. The flashlight would help him home in on her in the dark. He roared, launched himself, and loped after the light.

The woman heard the roaring tiger crash through the undergrowth as it chased her. She ran full pelt for the entrance of the village. Her house was three hundred feet away. "Aiieeeee," she screamed as she ran. "A tiger is after me."

The tiger loped into the village and loped after the fleeing woman. The woman ran on and burst through her door into her hut. She turned around to close it but the loping tiger burst in. The tiger hit the woman full pelt and the velocity of the heavy running body threw her again the shacks northern mud wall. She hit the wall and fell screaming to the ground. The tiger grabbed her right feet in his jaws and dragged her out of the shack. It let go of the legs, straddled the screaming woman and a smack on her face with his right forepaw stunned her into silence. The tiger roared, opened his mouth wide, drew his jaws around the neck, and jerked the head to the right snapping the neck bone. The woman lost consciousness. The tiger then lifted the neck and dragged the body out of the hut. He dragged the body down the single mud street and dragged it into the jungle and disappeared into the darkness.

Not a door in the village opened when the stricken woman had screamed. It was a case of every man for himself or every woman for herself. The encounter in the shack had been swift and silent. The headman's child lay sleeping on a bed of straw oblivious of the fact that his mother had been attacked and dragged away by a tiger.

T20 had truly gone rogue. He had gone berserk.

Chapter(6) Great white hunter

Henry Phibb's sat relaxed on the porch of the Bhim Bandh forest bungalow. The porch he sat in faced a second bungalow with a hot water swimming pool between the two buildings. The upper hills in the forest of Bhim Bandh were blessed with half a dozen hot springs. One spring emanated from the ground right at the head of the hot water swimming pool. The boiling water bubbled out of the ground in a round pool of about six feet radius and flowed into the swimming pool. That is how the pool got its daily supply of hot water.

There was a wooden table and half a dozen plastic chairs standing untidily at various places on the porch. Henry Phibb's sat on one of the chairs enjoying a Mc Dowels beer. His rifle lay on the table behind which he was sitting. It was an old world war two vintage German Mauser bolt action 303 rifle his father had brought back after the Second World War. The late Phibb's had enlisted in the British Indian army to add his bit to the war effort. He saw action in Africa and fought Rommel's Africa Corps under Montgomery. He found the rifle on a dead German soldier and took it as a souvenir. Henry had used it in quite a few hunting expeditions where he killed deer and wild pigs. That was when hunting wasn't banned by the Indian Government. After the ban, the rifle went into hibernation in his closet.

Today Henry was dressed elegantly in a pair of blue jeans and a white and blue checked cotton shirt. He had accepted the forest department's offer, left Elizabeth behind to look after the fish farm, taken a Tonga to the railway station, and caught the train from PUSA railway station to Bhim Bandh's nearest station. It was Jamui railway station. A forest department Jeep was waiting for him at the railway station with two eager forest officers and Ram Singh sitting in the vehicle.

So Phibb's was now ensconced in this lovely forest bungalow which he had forced the forest department to construct during his stint as a forest officer in Bhim Bandh. He had come three days ago and had visited the spots where T20 had killed humans. He didn't see any remains or left over's of the dead victims as the remains had been collected and cremated. Till then T20 had executed 40 human kills out of which ten were wood cutters. This struck him as natural. Historically, lonely wood cutters were an easy target for man eaters.

Henry knew T20 well. He knew him since his birth and his life as a cub. He was part of a litter of two cubs. One was T19 and the other was T20. He had seen T19 yesterday. T20 was not to be seen. The latter had been a normal tiger in the habit of hunting for prey in the river. The last thing Henry expected was one day T19 or T20 would kill humans.

The forest department's watchman who was on duty at the Bungalows entrance gate told Henry about the three boys who had come with a gun and three girls on a picnic and had shot and injured T20. "Henry sahib," the watchman had said. "I studied some of the kills. T20 never gouges out the meat from the rump as tigers usually do. I believe T20 doesn't have his canine teeth."

Henry Phibbs sipped his beer as he contemplated. He heard the roar of a Jeeps engine and looked to his left. It was a brand new vehicle belonging to the forest department. It was in stark contrast to the old world war two vintage Ford Jeep that stood parked further away and which he used in his frequent forays into the Jungle. Ram Singh was behind the new Jeeps wheels. He braked in front of the porch, switched off the ignition, stepped out of the Jeep, ran up the flight of four steps and walked excitedly to where Henry was sitting. The latter stood up. "Hello Ram Singh. What's the excitement all about?" he asked.

"T20 has killed a human. He killed a woman."

"Where?"

"In the village of Barhi. It is twenty kilometers from here. Sir, I think we should give the kill a visit while it is still fresh. T20 might come back to it."

Henry stood up and picked up the Mauser from the table. The rifles magazine was on the table fully loaded with six 303 bullets. Another half a dozen bullets lay scattered on the table. He had taken them out of their hibernation in his closet and was drying them in the sun. Henry collected the bullets and shoved them in his right trouser pocket. The magazine went into the breast pocket of his shirt. Accompanied by Ram Singh he walked to the edge of the porch and walked past Ram Singhs Jeep. Ram Singh was perplexed. "Sir this is your Jeep. It is for you. Where are you going?"

Henry turned around and pointed at the open hoodless old world war two Ford Jeep that was parked further away. It was used by the bungalow staff and he had used it the last three days. It still had the faded olive green color of the American army. "I will travel on that Jeep." Henry said as he walked towards the vehicle.

"But that is an old Jeep. It may break down on the way. Sir, this is a brand new Mahindra and Mahindra Jeep."

Henry stopped, turned around and smiled. "I feel at home in this Jeep. It is a Ford Jeep, an old American Jeep in India. I am an old American in India. That is the connection. It is my only connection to an unknown home my ancestors left behind."

Ram Singh smiled and walked past his Jeep. He made a sign to his driver who obeyed and ran into the bungalow and emerged with some keys. He handed one to Ram Singh.

Ram Singh took the keys and climbed into the driver's seat of the old Ford Jeep. Henry climbed into the passenger seat and laid his rifle on his lap. Ram Singh switched on the Jeeps ignition causing the vehicle to cough and roar to life. He pressed the clutch, meshed the gears, let go of the clutch, and pressed the accelerator. The Jeep was off. It roared out of the bungalow compound, turned right, and roared down the dirt track that meandered through the forest.

Ram Singh started a conversation while he drove. "Last night T20 executed his forty first victim," he said as he steered the old American vehicle along the forest road. "A group of woman had gone to defecate in the Jungle at night. One of them was attacked and killed. It was the village headman's wife."

Henry shrugged. He knew the Hindu's well. They were very conservative and particular about concealing their women folk's vanity. Women had to defecate in the privacy of the night. This was the unwritten rule in most Indian villages that did not have toilets. Men defecated in the fields, river side, or pond side during the day while the women defecated after dark. The sad part about the killing was that all the villagers in the villages in and around Bhim Bandh forest had been alerted and warned about the man eater. But wood cutters and midnight defecators were still falling victim to the tiger.

"The forest department will have to instruct the villagers about T20's habits. Number one," Henry said. "Till date he has killed ten wood cutters and ten night time defecating women. That means it has made it a habit to lurk in the vicinity of villages, choose its target, and attack it in the seclusion of the forest."

Ram Singh nodded his head as he honked the Jeeps horns at a bullock cart. The bullock cart left the road allowing the Jeep to speed on.

"I would like to have a meeting with the villagers," Henry said. "I would like to instruct them on how to defend themselves if a tiger attacks."

"How do you expect them to protect themselves without firearms?" Ram Singh asked.

The Jeep jerked and roared on as Henry continued the discussion. "I agree it is tough to protect yourself from a man eating tiger without firearms," Henry said. "But we have to impart basic knowledge of tigers to them. They will have to use whatever they have at their disposal."

The Jeep roared on as its occupants discussed T20. It travelled for half an hour bucking, skipping, and bouncing over obstacles giving the old American a hard time. It neared the village so Ram Singh stopped the vehicle and switched off the ignition. Henry looked around. The Jeep was standing in a section of the road in a valley between two forested hills. Henry looked into the valley below the road. It was thickly forested with the thatched roofs of huts visible in the distance. "Is that the village?"He asked.

"Yes sir," Ram Singh replied as he climbed out of the vehicle as Henry climbed down from the other side. The two walked twenty feet up the road and saw a path veer off the road and enter into the jungle to their right. Ram Singh motioned to Henry to follow. The latter walked away from the Jeep. He pulled out the loaded magazine from his breast pocket and shoved it in the slot in the rifles breach. Holding the rifle with the barrel pointing to the ground Henry followed Ram Singh.

The two left the road and carefully walked down the Jungle path. They disturbed a peacock in the midst of its so called dance. The bird closed its plumes and scampered into the Jungle. The men walked on as they pushed aside branches, leaves and ferns that grew over the path. They soon reached the base of the hill which also happened to be the floor of the valley. They could hear the gurgling of a stream nearby.

"It sounds like a forest stream," Henry said. Sure enough, the path led to a stream. They forded the stream and crossed to the other side soaking the lower part of their trousers and their keds. The narrow path carried on into the forest so they walked along it.

"Sir, we have reached the village," Ram Singh said as he walked into open land. Henry walked up and stood beside him. It was a filthy looking village with mud walled huts and thatched roofs and a single mud floored alley running between the huts. The alley was pock marked with slushy pot holes. The village had no drains. Domestic waste was simply thrown out of huts into the alley. The two men walked down the alley and walked past the huts as men and women came out to see who the intruders were. They recognized Henry and the forest officer.

The two walked to the middle of the village which was a big patch of land under the shady bowl of a huge banyan tree. A group of people were assembled under the tree and were listening to the headman whose wife had been killed by the tiger last night.

The headman saw the forest officer and Henry approach so he stopped speaking and folded his hands in a Namaste to the two.

Ram Singh and Henry walked up to the group and picked their way through the group and reached the headman. "Someone please fetch a chair if it is available," he said to the villagers who were all sitting cross legged on the dirt floor.

The villagers shook their heads. None of them owned a table or chair. Neither did any of them know anyone who owned a table or chair. So Henry had to make do by remaining standing.

Ram Singh addressed the crowd. "I think you all know Henry sahib?" he said. "He has come here to help us rid ourselves of the tiger."

The villagers looked hopefully at Henry as the village headman started sobbing. "Sahib, please kill the tiger," he said. "It killed and ate half of my wife."

Henry stared down at the villagers sitting on the ground before him. He spoke in perfect Hindi. "I would like to first give you people some advice. Now, till the tiger is killed, you must be prepared to defend and protect yourself. Arm yourself with anything. Make sure you have a spear or axe or sword or any sharp long thing nearby any time of the day."

The villagers nodded their heads.

Henry continued. "And remember, animals are afraid of fire. And if the tiger does attack you in the village, nobody will run. United, all of you will stand. Divided, one of you will fall. Get together and make a ruckus.

Yell tiger, tiger, and alert the others. If you run, it means that you have let down your guard and your only weapon to scare it. I know what I am going to say may sound foolish. But it is a fact. You are totally at the tiger's mercy if you run. Don't run. Don't think you can outrun the tiger and run away. It has more stamina and more speed than you."

The villagers nodded their heads. Everyone was concentrating on what Henry was saying.

"Your only option left is to either climb onto something high, like a tree which a tiger cannot climb, or fight back."

The villagers stared at Henry.

"Your only option left is to fight. And you must fight," Henry continued. "Whether you like it or not, that is your only hope to survive. I know it is slim. But it is there. Try to hit it with whatever you got on the face, especially on the snout. That is its weak part. And remember, if a tiger enters a village, everyone will attack it from all sides. Hit it with sticks, stones, bamboo spears, swords or any sharp thing. Make an awful lot of noise. Believe me, you will scare it and cause it to run away."

The villagers nodded their heads.

"If crackers are available, then burst them. Tigers are afraid of loud bangs. Beat drums and tin cans and anything noisy which you can get your hands on. Make a ruckus like what you do during the Diwali festival. It will get confused and scared and will be forced to run away."

The villagers nodded their heads.

"Now will some of you lead me to the dead body?" Henry asked.

The sobbing headman intruded. "White sahib, there is no dead body. We retrieved whatever remained of my wife and cremated it on the banks of the river."

"That's unfortunate," Henry replied. 'It would have returned to eat more of its kill. I could have a go at capturing it or taking a shot at it."

Ram Singh was concentrating on the crowd so he turned to address Henry. "Sir, we will have to make use of a goat."

Henry nodded his head in agreement. "Yes, we'll have to use a goat. If it returns to finish off its meal, it will certainly attempt to kill the goat. I will take a shot at it then."

"I have a goat," the village headman said. "I will give it to you if it helps in killing the tiger."

"Yes, bring it over," Ram Singh said.

The village headman scampered off so Henry continued. "I understand that most of you are wood cutters?" he asked.

The villagers nodded their heads.

"Do you have mirrors?"

"None of the villagers had mirrors. It wasn't necessary to keep mirrors. A mirror was regarded as a luxury in the village. The women folk had long hair, but they hardly combed it and simply tied it in a bun. That is why Ram Singh thought they looked slovenly. Even if some of them did comb their hair, the combing was done without a mirror.

Henry realized this so he nodded his head. "Now I want each of you to visit the nearest bazaar and buy yourself a mirror."

"Why a mirror?" a bare backed villager who was sitting cross legged on the ground asked. "Will the tiger admire itself in the mirror and say oh what a handsome tiger I am."

The villagers burst out laughing.

Henry was serious. "Stop laughing," he said sternly. "It is important that everyone keeps a mirror with him when he goes into the jungle. Ten wood cutters were killed by the tiger. When you chop a tree, always hang the mirror on the tree you are chopping. The mirror must be in front of you so that you can occasionally glimpse into it and see what is behind you. Remember, a tiger prefers to stalk from the back. It will target your neck, so tie a thick cloth around your neck when you go into the jungle. And when you chop wood keep glancing into the mirror. This will help you to stay alive. And while you are chopping, and if you do happen to see a tiger in a mirror creeping up towards you, don't panic and run. Be cool. If you run, it will easily chase you, outrun you, and kill you. Either climb up a tall tree as tigers don't climb trees or continue chopping wood with your eye on the mirror. Don't take your eyes off the tiger in the mirror. Your life will depend on that. When it comes close enough to you, without warning, instantly turn around and slam its face with your axe. Hit the face and aim at the snout. The axe is a heavy weapon. If swung with full force it has the capacity of breaking the tiger's skull, and if you hit the snout, it will at least stun the tiger and maybe split the face thereby killing it. But that needs a lot of courage, and this is your only option."

The villagers nodded their heads.

"White sahib," a villager said addressing Henry. "We apologize for laughing. You speak with brains and we laugh without brains."

Henry smiled. "That's okay," he said as he looked up. The bare backed headman had arrived with a black colored nanny goat in tow.

"Sahib, will this goat do?"

"Take me to your house where the tiger attacked your wife," Henry said as he turned to Ram Singh. "And could you ask the villagers to make some sort of platform. We need a flat contraption to sit the night out in a tree."

Ram Singh turned to address the villagers while Henry followed the headman. He followed him down the filthy alley picking his way through the slush to the first house on the right hand side of the entrance to the village. Sure enough there were pug marks on the ground near the doorway of the shack. He walked up to a pug mark and knelt down to study it. There were splotches of dry blood nearby.

Henry stared at the imprint in the mud and looked for a slight line down the side of the tiger's right forepaw. He found it. It was a healed cut the tiger had received as a cub from a sharp material in the jungle. The killer was T20 no doubt. The pug mark belonged to him.

Henry stood up as Ram Singh and the villagers walked up. A villager was holding a chachri. It was a bamboo platform made of slit bamboo hammered side by side to each other with nails. The villagers perched this platform on forks of branches of trees to sit on when they themselves went hunting.

"Though the contraption looks uncomfortable, this will do," Henry said. "Now take me to where you found the dead body of the woman." Henry looked at Ram Singh and added. "And you bring the goat along," he told the village headman.

The little group walked into the jungle leaving the village behind. They followed a path through the foliage. There was no need to go tracking along the route the tiger had taken when it dragged the dead woman away. The headman had done the tracking in the wee hours of the morning and found the mutilated half eaten body. He was now taking Henry directly to the spot where he found the body.

The group pushed their way through leaves, ferns, and branches, and after trudging through a kilometer of jungle, they reached the spot the headman had found his dead wife. "This is the spot sahib," he said.

Sure enough there were drops of blood on the ground and on some magnolia bushes. Bits of cotton sari cloth and female hair were entangled in the bushes.

Henry surveyed the area around the bush. He looked for a tree.

It was the village headman that chose a tree. "That tree is a good enough place to sit and wait for the tiger," the headman said as he pointed at a Peepal tree twenty feet away. It was a tall tree with a branch which forked into two. The fork in the branch was a perfect place to support the bamboo platform or chachri.

Henry approved of the tree. "Yes, seat the chachri on the branch," Henry said. He then turned to the headman and ordered. "And tie the goat to that stub poking out of the ground."

The headman obeyed, bent down, and tied the goats tether to the wooden stub which actually was a sub root that branched off the Peepal tree's main root. He stood up and with the help of a villager carried the bamboo platform to the base of the Peepal tree. He placed the platform down on the ground and clambered up the tree to the forked branch. It was fifteen feet above the ground so was safe enough for a human to sit and wait in ambush. Sitting on his haunches the headman made a sign to the villager to send the chachri up. The villager obeyed, and pushed the heavy chachri up the trunk of the tree. The headman sat on the branch, lay on it, reached down and took hold of the chachri. He hauled it up and placed it comfortably on the fork of the branch. Satisfied, he stood on his knees and crawled onto the chachri. It was a perfect platform.

The headman looked down at Henry.

Henry looked up and taking hold of his rifle by the butte he sent the rifle up so that the barrel was just under the chachri. "Here take my rifle and put it on the chachri," Henry said.

The headman lay flat on his stomach on the platform and lowered his hand to grab the rifle barrel. He took hold of the barrel and hauled the rifle up. Henry climbed up the trunk, crawled onto the branch, crawled onto the chachri, and sat cross legged next to the headman. "Ram Singh, take the villagers and go back to the Jeep. Bring back my breakfast in the morning. This man and I will wait here till morning and see if T20 comes back searching for its kill."

Ram Singh nodded and motioned to the villagers to follow him. The group of humans walked away leaving Henry and the headman to themselves.

It was soon dark and Henry got a shock. He had forgotten his flashlight. With age, he realized he had become forgetful. "I forgot to bring a torch," Henry said.

"I have one sahib. I always keep a torch with me in the jungle," the headman said as he fished out his flashlight from a fold of his dhoti.

"Keep it, it will prove handy," Henry said. "I've grown old. Imagine it. I'm on a tiger hunt and I haven't brought a torch with me."

The two waited into the night. They watched as fireflies took over the jungle as though there were hundreds of stars right in front of them. Glow worms lovingly replied to the fireflies by glowing on the ground as though the stars had come down. They heard the lonely hooting of an owl and the cry of cicadas. A jackal's lonely cry and the whistle of breeze amongst the leaves made the headman feel as though his dead wife was crying out to him for revenge. "My dear husband, help me. Kill the tiger," she seemed to say.

The goat suddenly started bleating. Henry and the headman became tense. They peered into the dark. The goats bleating continued and after a minute of bleating it was accompanied by a snort, then a grunt. The two peered at the tree base below them and realized the grunting had grown louder. There was rustling in the bushes to their right causing them to shift their gaze to the right. The grunts graduated to a loud squeal and a wild pig broke out of the undergrowth. It looked at the bleating goat, sniffed the air in front of it, squealed, turned around, and rushed back into the jungle.

Jungle night sounds once again took over the environment and, sitting on the platform, the two humans dozed off. Nothing disturbed them or approached the goat that was nibbling at the grass below them. Henry and the headman continued sleeping.

At precisely two AM Henry woke up. The goat was once again bleating loudly. He was lying beside the headman who was asleep so he silently turned over and lay on his stomach as he peered through the bamboo slits at the ground below. He saw the goat in the moonlight but nothing else. The goat was looking in the direction of some bushes and bleating its heart out. The bushes suddenly parted and a grunting wild boar waddled out. It grunted, sniffed the air, got the humans smell, grunted again, and scampered into the jungle to its left. The humans scent had scared it.

Henry waited quietly for a couple of hours before sleep overtook him and he quietly dozed off again. As he lay half asleep it struck him that all of T20's victim's remains were collected and cremated straight after the kill. T20 usually did not have the remains of his kills to return to so most probably he was now in a habit of not returning to his kills. T20 was a problem.

Chapter(7) The drunk grass cutter

The village of Bidupur was nestled on the north facing slope on a forested hill twenty miles to the south of Bhim Bandh forest bungalow. It was a simple cluster of mud and thatched roofed huts on the hillside. There was no street or no village square. The people eked out a living by collecting Tendu leaves from Tendu trees which was supplied to businessmen in the nearby town of Jamui to be made into plates to eat in during feasts. North India had a history of eating from these leaf plates during feasts and religious ceremonies.

Five hundred meters to the right of the village the hillside caved in allowing a stream bed with a stream to flow down the hill. This stream was the village's source of water. And today the stream had a visitor. It was T20. The tiger bent down low to slake his thirst. He was hunched over his fore paws while his tongue noisily lapped up water. It was three days since his last kill and he was hungry.

After slaking his thirst, he crossed the stream to the other side and slunk into some bushes. He peered through the leaves in front of him at the thick forest greenery beyond. A monkey chattered above his head. The latter had informed the animal world about the tiger.

T20 stepped forward and moved noiselessly through the bushes. He disturbed a myriad of insects and little creatures that lived in the undergrowth. Grass hoppers hopped away, trap door spiders disappeared into their traps, while spiders climbed up their own silk webs. T20 ignored the world he had disturbed and walked with lolling tongue as he panted. A jungle hare got a surprise and hopped away. Squirrels scampered up a tree.

T20 continued walking silently through the undergrowth till he reached the hillside and the village which was nestled half way up the hill and was surrounded by the jungle. He turned right and climbed uphill for three hundred feet till he reached a spot directly above the village. He sat down on his haunches and peered through the leaves as he studied human activity below him. He was going to choose a target.

The tiger watched some children playing in the narrow alleys between the huts. He watched women washing clothes or cooking food in front of their huts. Some men and women were busy arranging broad green Tendu leaves the villagers had fetched from the forest, into neat little stacks. They tied the stacks with ropes and prepared themselves to carry the load down the hillside all the way to the distant highway. Domestic pigs grunted and wallowed in the village's filth. The breeze was in the tigers favor so the grunting animals were unable to get the tigers scent.

T20 sat there in the bushes for a whole hour contemplating on what he would do. He was hungry so he waited for another half hour after which he silently stood up. Crouching low, he slunk out of the underbrush and still crouched, he stealthily went down the hill. Step by cautious step he meandered through shrubs and bushes on his way down meandering around tree's and protruding rocks. He was headed towards a woman who was cooking food in front of the first hut that was amongst the first rung of huts at the edge of the forest. When he was approximately twenty meters above her, he burst out of the bushes and loped down the hillside towards the woman.

The woman saw him crash out of the undergrowth and bound down. She screamed and ran down the hill, past her shack, to the middle of the village screaming, "tiger, tiger, tiger."

T20 loped in after her and was not ready for the solid smack he received on the face from a bamboo pole. Henry Phibb's had visited the village and instructed the villagers on how to fight back. He had sternly told them not to run away. Never.

The woman's screams of 'tiger' had brought about a spontaneous reaction from the villagers. They grabbed any tool they could get hold of and ran in the direction of the screaming woman. Each and every man in the village was holding a crude bamboo spear and was hollering at the tiger at the top of his voice as he ran. They saw the tiger lope behind the woman and headed straight for it. The village headman was the courageous one. That is why he had been elected the village headman. He was the first to swing his bamboo pole at the tiger and smack it on its face thereby angering it and causing it to turn its attention to him.

T20 received the smack and hopped around to face the attacker. He roared and charged only to receive half a dozen more blows on the face knocking him down sideways on the ground. He reacted with lightning speed and sprang at an attacker only to receive more blows causing him to spring a few feet back and snarl at the wildly yelling villagers. The tiger was now scared and confused. The din came from every direction as the whole village was brandishing bamboo poles, yelling at the tiger, and beating tin cans making a huge noise. The pointed ends of the bamboo poles were pointed at the tiger.

The tiger growled and prowled around in a circle warding off an occasional jab from a spear with its paw.

"Kill it, tear it apart," women of the village shouted as they beat tin cans with sticks adding their bit to the din.

Someone lit a firecracker and threw it at the tiger. It burst three feet in front of the confused animal. T20 roared, turned around, and attacked the bamboo holders behind it. Another fire cracker was thrown at the tiger. It burst two feet behind the stricken animal. The tiger braved the bamboo poles and sprang at an attacker who lunged at it with the pole. The pointed end of the pole grazed the tigers face and the latter landed squarely on the man. The man was desperate. He panicked and kicked up from under the tiger as the other villagers screamed and swung or jabbed their poles at the tiger. The animal received multiple blows but somehow managed to scare some humans into leaving an opening. It roared, paralyzing the stricken man under it as it received half a dozen more blows. It roared, sprang forward and loped off with the shouting screaming villagers chasing it. It loped up the hillside past ramshackle shacks and screaming women till it disappeared into the undergrowth above the village. The villagers saw the disturbed ferns, bushes, and other foliage shudder and shake as the tiger passed through. The shaking foliage showed the route the tiger had taken.

The villagers stopped at the spot their village ended and the jungle tree line started. They had successfully warded off the tiger. The American hunters lecture had come in handy and helped them protect themselves. No one had run away. Each and every male in the village had picked up a sharp object and attacked the tiger thereby scaring it off. They did not follow it into the jungle as it would be risky chasing it or looking for it in the forest foliage. They would be dispersed and out of each other's view. They would be vulnerable in the jungle if the tiger attacked. So the excited villagers walked back down the hill to the village. They had successfully warded off the dreaded man eating tiger of Bhim Bandh.

While the villagers gathered in the village square to excitedly discuss today's success and the woman's lucky escape due to their courage, two hundred meters up the hill, T20 had stopped and was peering down the hillside at the village. He was surprised and confused. The villager's reaction was most unexpected. He had expected them to run which was usually what happened when he attacked. Instead the humans had attacked him and scared him off with firecrackers. He was afraid of the noise they made. It was too loud and rang in his ears. It was unnaturally loud. He looked down at the village and realized he didn't have the courage to enter it a second time.

A peacock that was sitting on a Jamun tree fifty feet up the hillside noticed the tiger. It was surprised. "Kwa-aa-kwa-aa-kwa-aa," it called out. The call was picked up by another peacock that was sitting in a horse radish tree. The sound seemed to pierce the ear. A chital hind somewhere in the forest picked up the call and soon the forest echoed with the frequent and frenzied calling of animals informing each other of the presence of the tiger. Birds took to flight and fluttered and squawked and flew in circles above the tiger causing the villagers to look up. They knew what the commotion was all about.

T20 decided to leave the area. He knew that he had given away his position and it would be impossible to hunt in this area. Both the humans and animals had been alerted of his presence, so he turned around and soundlessly slunk into the foliage walking in a straight line around the hill. He travelled noiselessly among the greenery making sure the birds in the sky could not see him.

He reached the stream in which he had earlier slaked his thirst two hours ago. He once more hunched himself on his forepaws and lapped up some water. His face hurt where the bamboo poles had hit him.

T20 waded across the stream and entered the jungle on the other side. He walked on towards a neighboring village. He was hungry and had lost energy chasing the woman down the hill and loping up the hill to escape the humans. It was necessary for him to kill and devour a human or anything as big as a human. The village he had left behind was alert of his presence and it would be futile for him to attempt to kill a human there. He would try his luck in another village.

The neighboring village was two miles away. And today was a lucky day for T20. A group of women were preparing to go out into the jungle to cut grass for their cattle. They lived in the village called Chanan which was nestled in the middle of the forest in a broad valley which resembled the plains. It was a well to do village by Bhim Bandh standards and was in the middle of a two hundred acre paddy field. The villagers had illegally cleared the jungle and engaged themselves in various agricultural activities on the land. That is why the village was a wee more prosperous than those on the hillside.

And with prosperity comes alcohol. Jitan Ram was a drunk. He was perennially drunk. He owned five cows which gave him around twenty liter's of milk a day which he sold in the town of Jamui. At the rate of forty rupees a liter, he averaged a daily income of eight hundred rupees a day. With the going labor rate of one hundred and fifty rupees a day, eight hundred rupees a day was a royal income fit for a king in rural India. It was a win win situation for Jitan Ram, a one hundred percent profit as

Jitan Ram never bought fodder to feed his cows. His cows ate for free in the jungle. The whole jungle was their larder with all sorts of plants to chew and eat on. That is why his cows were healthy, that is why they gave quality milk, and that is why Jitan Ram got a good price in the market. It was easy money.

The problem in rural India, or in forested India, was that there is no outlet to enjoy or splurge your money in. No clubs, no discos, no restaurants, no cinemas or multiplexes, only the sleazy dhaba's on the highway in the distance. And the sleazy dhaba's got the bulk of their profit from alcohol.

That is why Jitan Manjhi would go daily to Jamui, sell his milk, buy alcohol, and other essentials and come back home drunk. He would come back with bottles of alcohol resulting in him drinking the whole day and the whole night. It was amazing how his liver withstood the steady flow of alcohol in his system.

The only time he wasn't drinking was when he was cutting grass. Today was no exception. As usual Jitan Ram was drunk. He generally took his cows out into the jungle, but last month the jungle had devoured a cow. A costly Jersey cow was bitten by a cobra while it was grazing. The cow died and the drunk was devastated by the loss. The cow's death now meant that he would sell five liters of milk less than what he sold daily. At the rate of forty rupees a liter he daily lost two hundred rupees. Another cow lost could entail another two hundred rupee loss a day. And the drunk didn't want that so he decided not to send his cows to graze in the jungle. He would himself accompany the female grass cutters into the jungle and cut and bring back two baskets of grass.

The drunk picked up the baskets from the middle of the mud floor of his shack. He stepped out into the bright sunlight and blinked his eyes. A sickle was in one of the baskets, so, fully equipped to cut grass he staggered forward. His right leg left the road and went up sideways as his body tilted to the left with his left leg taking the body load. The drunk somehow managed to straighten himself and put his right leg down on terra firma only to realize that his left leg had gone up with his body tilting slightly to the right. The drunk straightened himself and with his legs disobeying him and behaving oddly, he staggered past his cows into an alley between two rows of mud walled thatched huts.

The drunk walked on and walked into a bunch of half a dozen hens which were pecking at the ground. They seemed to move in circles as they pecked. One brown colored one unknowingly pecked its way to him causing him to give the hen an irritated kick. The hen squawked, fluttered its wings, and scampered off to the right. The other hens got the drunks message and scampered out of the way. The drunk was in a nasty mood.

The drunk staggered on and caught up with the group of sixteen female grass cutters who were also headed into the jungle. Trailed by the drunk, the little group left the village behind, and walked along the embankment of a paddy field till they reached a path that lead into the jungle. It was a narrow path which travelled along a narrow clearing which traveled above the path. The women automatically fell in line and walked up the path in single file. The drunk of course trailed the group and brought up the rear. He was finding it hard to keep up with the women.

The women chattered as the chatted amongst themselves as they walked along the path. They walked for half a mile into the jungle and turned right at an intersection. On the way they enjoyed a hearty snack of plums and berries which they plucked from nearby bushes as they walked.

The drunk dragged himself along somehow managing to walk. He was relieved when he realized the group had reached an area which was actually a grassy clearing. Someone had cleared the jungle of trees. That someone unknowingly allowed grass to grow in abundance to supply the village's cattle with fodder. The women put their baskets down on the ground and sat on their haunches and proceeded to cut grass with sickles they had brought along. They sang songs and chatted amongst themselves as they sliced through tufts of grass and put the tufts in the basket.

The drunk did not relish sitting and cutting grass amongst the female sex. It was considered unmanly so he staggered to the furthest corner of the opening near some thorny plum trees where the grass was the thickest. He dropped his baskets, sat on his haunches, retrieved his sickle, grabbed a tuft of grass, sliced through the tufts base and dumped the grass in the basket. He continued cutting the grass and dumping it into his basket. He didn't know he was being keenly watched by a pair of greedy hungry eyes from the hillside two hundred feet above him.

T20 was hidden in the foliage above the drunk and was watching him intently. He had been chased and hounded out of one village. But this scene was an entirely different. It was a lone human away from a bunch of humans. And none of them sported long poles like the ones in the village from where he had just escaped. T20 regarded himself lucky. After being chased away from the other village, T20 had made a beeline through the jungle to the drunk's village. He had stayed well hidden in the foliage studying the village for movement and was elated at the sight of the female grass cutters leaving the village. Through recent experience he knew grass cutters and wood cutters were an easy target for him. That is why he had trailed the grass cutters to the clearing in which they were now cutting grass. It would be wrong to say that he had trailed them, when the truth was he had slunk through the forest parallel to them just thirty feet away keeping an eye on them. Occasionally birds did flutter or fly off while animals scampered in different directions when they saw T20 slink up as it approached. The chatting females did not have knowledge of jungle sounds and thought the fleeing birds and animals were doing the disappearing act because of their noisy walk through the jungle. The tiger had stalked them to the clearing and had gone up the hill to have a strategic view of them. It looked down and made its pick. He chose the drunken grass cutter who was sitting alone and cutting grass in the edge of the clearing.

The grass cutter was too drunk to realize the danger he was in. He had made the mistake of singling himself out of the crowd of women. He didn't understand why a peafowl was screaming at the top of its voice.

Neither did he realize that a host of other birds had sighted the tiger and were squeaking and squawking their irritation at it. It was the women who first realized that something was amiss. Something was wrong. The birds were creating a ruckus and half a dozen monkeys were chattering to god knows whom.

"Why are the birds making such a lot of noise?" a grass cutter in a red sari asked.

"They have spotted a wild animal. I hope it isn't a tiger," said a grass cutter whose green sari blended perfectly with the foliage behind her.

The women stared up at the hillside and saw some movement two hundred feet up the hill. Red bottomed monkeys were hopping from tree to tree and screaming at something below them, showing it their teeth from the safety of their perch.

The undergrowth shook and burst open and to the women's horror they saw a tiger charge out. It was T20 who had launched his attack. The women screamed, threw down their sickles and ran down the path they had come. The drunk was left behind. He looked to the left at the fleeing women but his woozy brain did not allow him to connect to the reason why they were running away. It was by chance that he looked to his right and saw a yellowish haze rush down the hill charging and crashing through the undergrowth for all it was worth. His woozy mind still did not allow him to connect with reality. It was not until the tiger had dashed three quarters of the way down the hill that he finally connected to his predicament. "My god it is a tiger," he thought. Instinct of living his life in the jungle pulled him out of his drunken stupor to the reality of the danger that was bounding down the hill. He realized that the day's quota of alcohol had sapped his strength so he did not have the strength to stand up and run. He shot off to his right on all fours as he knew he did not have time even to get up. He scrambled, then half loped, then half ran as his body gradually straightened till he was finally running. He ran full pelt towards a Peepal tree with the tiger loping full pelt just thirty feet behind him. The drunk approached the tree, gave a mighty leap and grabbed hold of a branch in a futile attempt to swing himself up. But he was too late. The tiger had launched itself at him. It had sprung and aimed its attack at the drunk's neck while the latter was still running. But the drunk had jumped, so instead of the neck it caught the drunk's feet in its mouth while it was in full flight in mid air as it tried to stop its own spring. The momentum of the tiger's spring and its weight had two effects on the drunk. The latter was forced to let go of the branch as he was wrenched away and the tiger was forced to let go of the leg due to its own body speed. Together the tiger and the drunken man cart wheeled once in mid air and landed in two loud thumps on the ground. Way above them red bottomed monkeys screamed in excitement as though they were telling the drunk. "I warned you, I warned you, now be prepared to die."

The desperate drunk reacted with lightning speed. He sprang up, grabbed the branch, and swung his leg in an attempt to swing it up out of danger. Unfortunately T20 was faster. He roared as he sprang and grabbed the drunk's right feet in his steel like teeth and pulled down.

"Help," yelled the drunk as he tried to pull himself up as the tiger tugged down in its attempt to pull him down. The pain in the drunk's ankle and right feet was excruciating. It was unbearable. He felt as though the tiger was ripping his leg off his torso. Not being able to bear the pain, the drunk let go and fell with a thump on the grassy ground. He was now flat on the ground with his feet in the tiger's mouth. The tiger pulled back dragging the drunk a couple of feet. He then let go of the ankle and straddled the screaming man. A slap from his forepaw silenced the screams. The drunk was unconscious. The tiger then wound up the one sided fight with his death sentence to the drunk. He grabbed the latter's gullet in his jaws and flicked his gullet holding head to the left and to the right thereby snapping the drunks neck. The drunk was now on his way to the happy drinking grounds.

Still holding the neck T20 dragged the body into the forest.

Chapter(8) Sitting over the kill.

Henry Phibb's was lying flat on the ground and peering through the bushes at an overturned basket sixty feet away. The basket was made out of thin strips of bamboo interwoven into each other. It was standing upside down with one end on the ground and the other end, which was visible to Phibb's, propped on a twelve inch long stick. A string was tied to the base of the stick and traveled all the way to the bushes behind which Phibb's was hiding. The string traveled through the bush right into Phibb's hand. There was a brick balanced on top of the basket. Phibb's smiled as he looked at his contraption. It was a trap to capture a bird, to be precise, to capture a dove for dinner tonight.

Phibb's was a practical man. He did not believe in using expensive bullets to kill birds or small game if he wanted to eat something special. He simply trapped them. The trap at which he was peering at through the leaves of a bush was designed to trap doves. Phibb's relished eating roasted dove. These weren't available back home in PUSA, but they were in abundance in Bhim Bandh forest.

The trap was simple. An Overturned basket with one end standing on a stick with a stick attached to the end which a trapper held. Wheat gram was spread on the ground under the basket. The wheat grains would attract doves who relished them. They would first flutter over and look at the contraption with suspicion. But hunger and an hour of strutting suspiciously around the basket would take its toll on their fear. Suspicion flew away into the jungle. Pecking at the ground, they would peck their way to where the wheat grain was. Here the lure of wheat grain got the better of their fear and they proceeded to peck under the basket as they feasted on the grain. At the precise moment the trapper would flick back the string flicking the stick away from under the basket. The basket would suddenly fall on the surprised dove who would find itself trapped inside the overturned basket.

Phibb's smiled as he saw two pigeon's flutter over and settle down on the ground near the trap. "Good boys," he whispered to himself. "Now go in and have your meal."

The pigeons pecked around while Phibb's waited patiently to capture his meal. They would occasionally stop pecking and look in the direction of the trap.

"Yes my dears," Phibb's whispered. "Slowly does it. There's a feast in there."

The doves pecked at the ground and fluffed up their feathers. Actually it was the male dove that fluffed up its feather. He did half a dozen circles and continued fluffing his feather as the female watched him. The male was dancing to attract the female.

"Hey pal, stop waltzing. This is no time to be wooing females," Phibb's whispered to himself. "This is eating time."

As though she had heard and understood the human, the female dove pecked at the ground and entered the area under the basket.

"Good girl," Phibb's whispered to himself. "You are intelligent. Why think of boys when good food is around."

The male dove un-fluffed its head and was about to follow the female under the basket when it stopped. The roar of a Jeeps petrol engine disturbed it. It was the second world war vintage Ford Jeep which the forest department was the proud owner of. Ram Singh was driving it and the speed at which the Jeep was approaching told Henry that Ram Singh had important news. He looked in the direction of his trap, at his doves, and realized that they were on the verge of flying off. One was under the basket while the male dove was partly in and partly out. It was now or never so Phibb's pulled the string back causing the stick supporting the basket to hop back. With no support, the basket fell down with an end falling on the male dove. The latter fluttered its wings and to Phibb's dismay, became the baskets support leaving an opening for the female dove to crawl out. She did just that. Hunched low on the ground, she crawled out and flew off. The male dove somehow extricated itself from between the ground and the edge of the basket and flew off. A dismayed Phibb's looked at his food fly away as he stood up. Ram Singh was a spoil sport.

The Jeep roared up and stopped in front of him. Ram Singh hopped off and walked up to Phibb's. "Sir, the tiger has made a kill," he said excitedly. "A drunken villager in a village twenty miles from here was killed by T20 two hours ago. If we hurry we may be able to have a shot at it while it is still near the kill."

"That's impossible," Phibb's said as he walked up to the passenger side of the Jeep and climbed in. "Tigers are voracious eaters. They eat fast. You said it killed the man two hours ago. Two hours is too long. It will have eaten and left. Anyway, let's go to the forest bungalow. I will have to collect my rifle."

Ram Singh nodded his head and walked over to the driver's side of the vehicle. He switched on the ignition, pressed the clutch, meshed the gears, released the clutch and put his right foot down on the accelerator causing the Jeep to speed off. It roared down the road to the bungalows compound gate where it turned left, entered the compound, and stopped in front of the swimming pool. Henry hopped off and ran up the stairs to the bungalow's porch. "Turn the Jeep around while I fetch my rifle and some bullets," he said.

Phibb's emerged from the room after two minutes holding the Mauser in his right hand. He walked down the steps and climbed into the passenger seat of the vehicle next to Ram Singh. Ram Singh switched on the ignition and the Jeep was soon trundling out of the forest bungalow compound. It turned left and traveled along the dirt track which meandered through the forest.

"Sir," Ram Singh said as he drove the old American vehicle. "The tiger attacked in two villages today. It was driven away by alert villagers in the first village. Instead of panicking and running away they fought the tiger and caused it to run away. The villagers did as you advised them and made a lot of noise. Even I heard them when I was at a distance. So the tiger left that village and killed in the neighboring village. It attacked some grass cutters and killed a male grass cutter. The fellow was drunk. This happened outside the village in the jungle."

Phibb's silently looked at the rutted road ahead of him. "Ram Singh I have grown old," he said. "I'm no more young. That night I stayed up over the goat was tiresome. I don't relish sitting perched on tree's for the whole night. Hunting at this age is ridiculous. It is affecting my health. Age is getting the better of me."

Ram Singh did not reply. He continued concentrating on the road as the Jeep roared on.

"I want to lead a relaxed life now. That is what my age demands of me. I don't want to spend nights smacking irritating mosquitoes all night," Henry said.

The Jeep broke out of the forest as the rutted track entered open ground and travelled through some paddy fields. The vehicle slowed down as it approached the village after which Ram Singh slowly guided it into the village's single street. He drove slowly not wanting to squash a stray chicken or a goat under the Jeeps wheels. The villagers were extremely poor. He did not want them to incur a loss because of his driving.

The Jeep turned a bend around a thatched hut and stopped. A crowd stood on the road before it. They were all either peering or trying to peer into the drunk's ramshackle hut. Some women were inside consoling the drunk's bereaved wife who wailed as she hollered her grief to the world beating both her breasts with her hand.

Phibb's climbed down from the Jeep and walked towards the crowd. Seeing the white man with the gun approach them, the crowd parted and made way. Phibb's walked to the entrance, bent down low and peered in.

It was packed from mud wall to mud wall with weeping wailing women so he straightened up and turned to Ram Singh. "Ask them if they retrieved the dead body?"

Ram Singh turned around and asked the question to the villagers who were standing behind him. They told him that the body wasn't retrieved. They were too scared to chase or follow the tiger. At the moment they did not dare go into the jungle as the tiger may still be around. Ram Singh translated this piece of news to Phibb's.

"Too bad. It means they don't know where the tiger took the body. Then we will have to do some tracking," Phibb's said. "Tell some of these men to take us to the place the tiger attacked the grass cutter. And yes, we'll need a platform on a tree to sit out the night and keep a watch over the kill. The thing they call a chachri."

Ram Singh told the villagers this. Two of them nodded their heads and rushed off. They came back three minutes later with the bamboo platform.

"Tell someone to take us to the sight of the kill," Phibb's said.

The villagers nodded their heads and ten able bodied men agreed to accompany Phibb's to the kill. So the little group trudged out of the village and followed the little pathway the grass cutters had followed in the morning. They walked through the Jungle pushing away branches, leaves, ferns, and little trees as they made progress towards the killing site.

The group walked silently and reached the intersection where they turned right. They soon reached the open patch of land where the woman had been cutting grass. Fifteen baskets and around a dozen sickles were strewn untidily on the ground.

"Where did the tiger come from?" Phibb's asked.

A tall bare backed dhoti clad villager pointed to the hill that was directly in front of them. "From up there," he said. "It came running down the hill. That's what the women say."

Phibb's walked to the middle of the open patch of land and looked around. Yes, there were signs of a struggle near some thorny bushes under a tree. The grass was flattened and there were blot's of blood in three places. Phibb's walked over to the flattened grass and looked down at it. The tiger had killed the drunk here under the tree. He noticed the drag marks on the flattened grass over which the dead body had been dragged. The drag marks lead into the foliage to the right so Phibb's stood up. He looked at the greenery towards which the flattened grass was headed. Sure enough, there were more than a dozen broken twigs. Something big had passed through the foliage.

Phibb's motioned Ram Singh to follow him into the foliage. "Take three men along. They will take turns to carry the chachri," he said. "We have got some tracking to do."

Ram Singh turned to the villagers and asked seven of them to return. Three would accompany them and would take turns to carry the chachri. Seven villagers said a respectful Namaste to the American, turned around, and left the open patch of grassland to enter the jungle on their way back to the village.

Phibb's motioned to Ram Singh as he slowly pulled back his rifle bolt, allowed a bullet from the magazine to pop up and face the barrel entrance. He pushed the bolt back causing the bullet to be pushed into place in the barrel. By pushing the bolt down he had cocked the Mauser. He made a sign to Ram Singh and the others to follow as he himself cautiously walked into the jungle entering the area between the broken twigs.

The tell tale drag marks on the ground, the drag marks on the grass, and the drag marks on loamy soil or the undergrowth, made it easy to track the tiger. Broken twigs and ripped off leaves informed Phibb's of the path the tiger had taken. But Phibb's was careful. He wasn't sure where the tiger was so he stopped and picked up seven stone chips in his hand. He put them in his shirt pocket as he slowly and carefully brushed some ferns aside and stepped forward. He kept pushing back leaves, branches and ferns as he gingerly moved forward with his eyes darting in every direction. The four men behind him were patient and careful. They understood the situation well. They were also scared. They were surrounded by thick foliage and the tiger could be anywhere. Ram Singh felt vulnerable as he followed Henry. He hoped to god that age hadn't rusted Henry's reflexes. The villagers who followed held knives in their hands.

Phibb's stopped when he saw a blood soaked white patch of cloth entangled in a thorny plum bush. It was a part of the dead drunk's dhoti which was most probably ripped off when the cloth got entangled in the thorny bush as the tiger dragged the body away. There were more blood splotches on the ground ten feet away.

Ram Singh felt eerie as he followed Phibb's. The jungle sounds frightened him. But it was his job to accompany Phibb's who had once been his superior officer. He couldn't afford to show Phibb's that he was scared.

Phibb's looked at some bushes. He was suspicious of them so he pulled out a stone chip from his breast pocket and threw it at the bush. A robin red breasted and a dove fluttered and flew off. A couple of chameleons with turret like eyes scampered off to the right.

Satisfied that a tiger couldn't be in the bushes if birds were sitting in it, Phibb's carefully walked through the bush on his way to the other side. He pushed some ferns and leaves aside and continued walking slowly while his eyes darted from the left to the right. The ground was clear. There was no tiger.

The group slowly moved on walking step after cautious step. A couple of brown colored Hoopoe birds were disturbed. They had been running around in circles and pecking at the ground. Seeing the human intrusion, they flicked open the crescents on their heads, opened their wings and took to flight as black and yellow assassin bugs scampered off.

Phibb's skirted a mud mound. It was actually a termite chimney. There were two other chimneys. Their mud mounds were intact but the chimneys were destroyed. Phibb's knew who had destroyed the chimneys. Bears, Sloth bears were common in this jungle and they relished termites. Their modus to capture termites was simple. Break down the tall protective chimney, shove the snout in, blow hard and suck up the termites.

The group left the termite mounds behind and walked very carefully for a hundred feet through low bushes and jungle foliage. They saw a cobra sitting wrapped in coils on a Jamun tree's branch. Phibb's grimaced and carried on as he followed the drops of blood, the drag marks, pieces of torn cloth, broken twigs and leaves. They walked for another fifty feet when Phibb's made a sign to the men behind him to stop. There was a clump of magnolia bushes thirty feet in front of him. His right hand slowly entered his shirt pocket from where he pulled out two stone chips. He threw both the chips at the clump of bushes. Half a dozen brown munia's fluttered and took to flight. Satisfied that there was nothing in the bushes, Phibbs continued his careful progress forward. He walked for fifty feet and stopped when he saw flies. They were buzzing over something in a cluster of magnolia and plum bushes.

Phibb's made a sign to Ram Singh to stop. With his right forefinger he made a sign towards the magnolia bushes. Ram Singh and the others understood and stood still as Phibb's threw a stone chip at the bush. This only aggravated the flies who buzzed higher increasing the high pitched note of their buzz.

There was something dead in the bushes but there was no tiger. But Phibb's was cautious. He wanted to enjoy the luxury of his retired life on the banks of his fish pond eating freshly caught grilled fish. He did not want to end it abruptly with a swat from a tigers paw. So he fished out two more stone chips from his breast pocket and threw them at the bush. Nothing happened so Phibb's moved carefully forward to where the flies were buzzing. He carefully and silently approached the bush followed closely by the scared Indians. When he was just five feet away he stopped. He could see the half eaten corpse. A cheek and half the face was torn off, some ribs protruded out of the rib cage showing the man's intestines as the stomach had been gouged out. Part of the man's rump had been chewed off. The sight was unbearable for Ram Singh who realized his own stomach had been disturbed. He slumped to the ground and vomited. Phibb's was surprised at the forest officer. He disliked people with weak stomachs. But he did not have the time to scold the officer. His eyes were busy darting around making sure the tiger wasn't around as his fore finger rested on the Mausers trigger like a hook.

Ram Singh continued vomiting as the two villagers held his arm. "The sight was gory," he gasped. "I never saw a mutilated human body before. And hope I'll never see one again."

"Pull yourself together!" Phibb's whispered. "This will not do. You are a forest officer."

"But sir, I'm also human."

Phibb's glanced around him at the jungle and slowly walked over to the bushes and looked down at the mutilated mangled body. He turned when he heard a commotion behind him. A group of noisy villagers had followed them and were now walking towards Phibb's. One of them led a goat by the tether. The group was lead by a tall mustachioed man wearing a dhoti and kurta. He was the village headman.

The headman walked up to Phibb's and bent his head down low in a very reverent Namaste. The American accepted the Namaste with a polite hello.

"Sahib, we have come to collect the dead body for the cremation," the headman said.

Phibb's motioned him to stop and turned to Ram Singh who had stood up. "We need the body Ram Singh. Tell him that I will need the body if they want me to kill the tiger."

Ram Singh told the villagers about the request but the villagers argued with him. So ram Singh turned around to address Phibb's. "They say that it will be immoral of them to allow it to rot in the heat and be pecked by vultures. If you sit over it in the hope of the tiger coming back, flies and vultures and other carnivores will get a chance to devour it. They cannot allow that. It is immoral. They insist on taking the dead body away that is why they have a brought a goat along. They say you may use the goat as bait. Not their dead relative."

Phibb's was exasperated. "Look this is very selfish of them. I am a retired and tired old man and, hunting man eating tigers is no more my job. But I came here for their sake. I am at the moment risking my life when I should be luxuriating next to my fish pond. I am roaming around this jungle tracking a dangerous man eating tiger so that they can sleep peacefully in their homes. I am doing this for them thinking a human is helping some distressed humans. I had no business being here. Why should I be here? The least they can do is to help me. And they can help me by leaving the corpse here for one night. I'll make sure no wild animal will devour it."

Ram Singh turned around and told the villagers what Phibb's had just said. There was an argument after which an irritated Ram Singh turned back to face Phibb's and told him what the villagers had just said. The villagers also faced him but had their hands folded to the American in prayer.

"Sir, they refuse to cooperate," Ram Singh said. "They say that if they leave the dead body there in this state, then it will be regarded as a blot on their character and the character of the whole village. They are accursed if they leave it strewn around in its present condition. Whether you like it or not, they will take the dead body back to their village. You may have the goat."

Phibb's dropped his rifle on the ground and threw up his hands in exasperation. "I will never understand you Indians," he said. "Anyway, tell them to tie the goat to that root protruding from the ground under that Banyan tree."

The villagers looked to their right towards where Henry was pointing. There was a young banyan tree with branches branching out ten feet above the ground.

"Put the chachri neatly on the fork," Phibb's said as he pointed to a fork in the branch.

The villagers led the goat to the base of the tree and tied the tether to a prop root that was hanging down. Two villagers climbed up the tree and motioned to their friends to send the chachri up. They pulled up the chachri and lay it on the forked branch to make the platform as comfortable as possible. They then asked for a rope which was thrown up to them. It was evening now and soon would become dark so they hurriedly tied the chachri firmly to the forked branch after which they climbed down from the tree. Two villagers had brought along a sack each with them. They looked at Henry and walked to where the body lay mangled in the bushes. They carefully and respectfully picked up the head and torso and put them into the gunny sack. They then picked up the half chewed bottom and legs and shoved them into the sack. They proceed to scrounge the bushes for bits and pieces of flesh. Satisfied that they had collected all that was collectable, they took their leave from Ram Singh and Phibb's and left.

Phibb's looked at Ram Singh and smiled. "So we are ready for tonight's ordeal," he said.

Ram Singh nodded his head as he looked around. Phibb's handed him the rifle and proceeded to climb onto the tree. He grappled up the trunk and reached the branch panting his heart out. Ram Singh smiled and held the rifle up by holding the butt. The barrel reached the branch so Phibb's took hold of the tip and hauled the rifle up. He then turned around and laid the rifle on the branch. He pushed the rifle forward and crawled up the branch, pushed the rifle forward again and crawled forward after it till he reached the bamboo platform. He gingerly crawled onto the platform testing whether it would take his load. Satisfied that it would, he relaxed and lay his rifle down. He motioned to Ram Singh to climb up so the latter grappled up the tree trunk and climbed onto the branch. He crawled forward on all his fours on the branch till he reached the bamboo platform.

"I'd like to make a request to you Ram Singh," Phibb's said as he lay down on the chachri and spread his legs. He wanted to snooze.

"Make the request sir."

"I no more relish sitting up the whole night in a tree over a tiger kill. I will take a nap while you sit and stay on guard. If you do happen to see anything suspicious, wake me up. I don't think the tiger will come back to the kill. Bhim Bandh is a small forest and every corner of this forest is easily accessible. The villagers are in a habit of taking away the kill the same day and cremating it. The tiger seems to know that. It knows that if it will come back it will find nothing. That is why it isn't coming back to its kill. So if you do see something suspicious you must wake me up. And if you also feel like closing an eye then don't hesitate to wake me up."

Ram Singh nodded his head and prepared himself for his night time ordeal. He had his flash light that was supplied by the forest department to him safely tucked in his pocket. He sat on the platform while Henry Phibb's slept. The daytime noises gradually receded and night time forest noises took over. An owl hooted in the distance while crickets called. Ram Singh heard the long eerie wail of a dog in the distance and watched as the synchronized flashes of fireflies took over the dark jungle. Their flashes were replied to by the glow worms on the ground. At around eleven thirty PM he heard the rustling of leaves nearby. Ram Singh peered down and shone the flashlight in the area of the rustling. He saw a pack of half a dozen jackals slink into the undergrowth and disappear. Ram Singh swung the flash light beam onto the goat. It was happily and peacefully nibbling at the grass under the tree. Ram Singh wondered whether the goat knew that it was being used as a tiger bait. He shrugged, switched off the torch, and allowed the fire fly flashes to rule the jungle darkness around him. Soon there was a multitude of flashes in the air, amongst the trees and leaves and on the ground. Ram Singh could hear the goat nibbling on the grass below. He heard the lonely howl of a jackal. It sounded eerie as though the soul of the murdered man was yelling at him for revenge. A shiver ran down his spine as he peered at the dark jungle around him. In the moonlight he could see the forest silhouette. He heard the lonely hoot of an owl, the cry of a cicada, and the lonely howl of a jackal again. A dog barked somewhere in the distance. Ram Singh presumed it was barking in the village he had left behind. He yawned and realized he was fighting off sleep. He yawned again, closed his eyes, opened them, closed them again and forced them to remain open. He shook his head to shake off the sleep. He realized he was feeling woozy in the head so, he opened his eyes once again and went to sleep only to get up at early twilight. He looked around and scratched his neck. He peered down at the goat. The latter was nibbling peacefully at the grass. It stopped nibbling and looked up at him as though it was saying. "The tiger didn't come. Let's go back to the village."

Ram Singh shook Henry. "Sir, get up," he said. "The tiger didn't come."

Chapter(9) A crashed bullock cart

T20 strode through the jungle like a king. He was the king. The animals in the jungle feared him. Even the supposedly invincible humans feared him. That is why he had stopped concealing himself when he roamed around the jungle. He had thrown caution to the wind. This resulted in birds singing frequently when they spotted him and monkeys chattering noisily informing forest beings of his whereabouts, causing fleet footed animals to do the disappearing act.

T20 wasn't interested in killing and eating fleet footed animals. Why crouch, and slink through ferns and bushes when the easily killed weak limbed humans were available. He now slunk and hid in bushes and under low trees only when he was stalking humans. They had proved an easy target for him.

Unknown to T20, three kilometers away in the town of Jamui, some laborers were loading grains of rice onto a bullock cart. The rice was to be distributed in the villages in and around Bhim Bandh forest reserve. There were twenty fifty kg rice bags on the rickety bullock cart which had a bamboo floorboard and a wooden axle. The vehicle was harnessed to two sturdy white colored bullocks. The bullock cart driver climbed onto the vehicle, sat down with his legs hanging down and kicked at both the animals' rumps. "Aha,ha," he yelled at the bullocks as he prodded their rumps causing them to move forward. "Ah-ha-ah-ha-aha."

The bullock carts wheels squealed and squeaked in jarring noises. That was because the technology of the vehicle was ancient. It was a part of India that was frozen in time refusing to modernize. The area where the hub rotated around the iron axle had no ball bearing. It was fitted by a simple iron bush which squealed and squeaked and made all sorts of crude grinding noises under the load the bullock cart was carrying. So it was ear irritating grinding and screeching noises that accompanied the bullock cart where ever it went.

The bullock cart driver kicked into both the bullocks' rumps to make the creaking vehicle move faster. He had to drop two rice bags before nightfall in every village he visited. That meant he would have to visit ten villages before he could call it a day. "Aha-aha-aha," he yelled at his animals and clucked with his mouth. "Cluck-cluck-cluck."

The bullock cart picked up speed. The grinding noise and the squeals and squeaks of the carts axle increased. The driver sat relaxed with his back propped on a rice bag. He heard the parp of a motor vehicles horn and the roar of a petrol engine behind him. The cart was ancient, and whoever designed it did not conceive the necessity of a rear view mirror. Maybe in ancient times motor vehicles did not exist and vehicles never overtook each other. So to see what was honking behind it, the bullock cart driver hopped out of the moving vehicle and looked back. He recognized the forest departments old Ford Jeep. As usual it was hoodless with its windshield lying on the bonnet. Ram Singh was sitting behind the steering wheel with Henry Phibb's sitting relaxed beside him. Ram Singh saw the bullock cart driver hop out of the vehicle and look back at him so he parped his horn at the driver and waved to him to leave the road and make way. The bullock cart driver understood the Jeep driver's urgency to overtake his vehicle so he crossed over to the front of his vehicle to the left hand bullock, grabbed the animal's horn and guided the creaking vehicle off the road onto the footpath that travelled alongside the road. The Jeep immediately overtook the bullock cart and roared on kicking up dust at the bullocks and the bullock cart behind it.

The bullock cart driver climbed back onto his seat on his slow moving squeaking vehicle and watched the Jeep disappear in the distance. He clucked and 'ha-haa'd' at the bullocks whenever he felt that they had slowed down or were on the verge of stopping.

The bullock cart continued squealing and squeaking as it travelled on the tarmac road for half an hour after which the road entered the jungle. The old vehicle squealed and squeaked its way into the forest. The bullock cart driver had heard of the man eating tiger and hoped it wasn't anywhere around the villages he would visit. He was a poor man with a family of four to feed. He had to do his work and couldn't afford the luxury of leaving his work to hide and cower in his house as most of the villagers in the villages in and around Bhim Bandh were doing. He had to ply his vehicle if he wanted to feed his family. This is why he was braving the man eater's territory to take food stuff to the different villages.

The bullock cart reached an intersection. A dirt road branched off to the left into the Bhim Bandh jungle. The bullock cart driver pulled the reins of the bullock which was to the left clucking and 'ha-haaing' to the creature. The animal understood and turned left. The bullock cart was soon trundling down a dirt track.

It was the bullock cart driver's daily job to travel on this road so he knew it well. He knew that after a kilometer of winding along the jungle road, it would enter the hills. There was a two kilometer climb where he would get off the vehicle and push it from the back to help the bullocks pull the cart up the road. This was the irritating part. But after the climb the road leveled off and meandered through the hills as it passed the different villages.

The bullock cart reached the climb so the driver got off the vehicle, went to the back and pushed hard. He clucked and shouted several 'ha-haa's' at the bullocks as he pushed from the back. The bullocks heaved and the cart squealed and screeched as it inched up the hill.

The bullock cart driver pushed and clucked, pushed and clucked, pushed and clucked for fifteen minutes till the ancient vehicle reached the top of the climb. The driver was perspiring so he picked up a corner of his dhoti and wiped his face with it. Panting loudly, he walked over to the front of the vehicle, climbed onto his seat, made himself comfortable, propped his back against a sack of rice, took the reins and kicked into the bullock's rump. "Aaa-haa," he shouted at the bullocks that obeyed him and moved forward forcing the cart to trundle on. "Aaa-haa."

Unknown to the bullock cart driver, a kilometer ahead T20 was slaking his thirst in a little forest stream. He was hunched over his forepaws as he lapped up water. He would change his hunting strategy today. It was easier than stalking humans near villages. He would stalk and hunt a human on the lonely dirt track above him.

Having slaked his thirst T20 stepped into the water. It wasn't deep and hardly covered his feet. He waded to the other side of the stream and entered the thick jungle foliage. He brushed past ferns, leaves, and twigs as he walked unhurriedly towards the road. The stream was in a valley so the tiger found himself walking uphill. His strength allowed him to negotiate the uphill path easily. He soon topped off onto the dirt road along which the bullock cart was trundling on its way to the different villages of the forest. The tiger crossed the rutted dirt track and entered the jungle on the opposite side. It once more climbed noislessly uphill with his padded feet helping him to walk soundlessly. He reached a spot fifty feet above the road and decided it was a good enough place to lie in ambush. Directly below him was two hundred feet of road which was visible to him, so he settled down on the ground to patiently wait with his tongue lolling as he panted.

T20 did not have to wait for long. He soon heard the squeals and squeaks of the bullock carts wheels as the vehicle approached. He waited patiently as he peered down at the road through the ferns. The sudden chatter of a monkey just twenty feet above him irritated him. The monkey had seen the tiger. The latter's chatter was picked up by a peacock further up the hill who called in loud 'kwa-aaa's' informing the forest beings of the whereabouts of the tiger. The peacocks call was picked up by the shrill shriek of a chital hind. The forest was now filled with frequent calling. The tiger was lucky most humans, including the bullock cart driver, did not understand jungle sounds.

T20 saw the bullock cart trundle into view. The rider sat on the cart and was holding the bullock's reins. "Aaa-haa-aaa-haa," he said as he clucked at the bullocks. "Aaa-haa.' The driver didn't know that the man eating tiger was watching him with greedy eyes.

T20 pricked up his ears and stood on all his fours. He was still hidden in the ferns. He crouched, twirled his tail, and let out a low growl. He slowly stepped into the ferns in front of him as he slunk his way down towards the road. He zig- zagged between branches and other obstacles till he was level with the road. He hopped across some bushes, stepped onto the road, and turned to face the bullock cart. The vehicle stopped as the bullocks and human stared petrified at the tiger.

T20 gave a mighty roar. It was as though he had challenged the bullock cart driver to a duel. He then crouched low, twirled his tail, snarled, crept forward and suddenly lunged and made to lope towards the bullocks. The terrified bullock cart driver was on the verge of hopping off the vehicle and running down the road. But his bullocks were quicker and did not give him the opportunity to hop off. They panicked, turned right, and ran taking the over loaded vehicle with them. The horrified driver tried to jump off but it was too late. The bullock cart was moving too fast. The panicked animals crashed into the undergrowth taking the cart along. They went over the edge of the hill and were now galloping downhill with the cart speeding behind them as they smashed, crashed, and burst through the undergrowth with the cart dancing wildly behind them. Bags of rice flew off the cart as the stricken driver somehow clung onto the madly skipping vehicle as the latter did a mad jig on its way down. The weight of the cart and its speed forced the harnessed bullocks to gallop at break neck speed. They galloped on downhill and hopped over some rocks. The carts wheels hit the rocks and bounced off lifting the rear of the cart over the galloping bullocks as it cart wheeled and landed with a thump on the rider who hung on to the vehicle which was now above him with the wheels spinning near his head. The bullocks continued their mad run down the hill taking the overturned cart along with them. They were galloping too fast so they slipped, fell, and somersaulted through the undergrowth with the empty cart, cart wheeling behind them. The cart was headed straight for a Peepal tree as the driver was thrown off and rolled down the hill.

The bullocks rolled down the hillside past the Peepal tree as they crashed through the undergrowth. The bullock cart hit some rocks causing its downward momentum to throw it up in the air and cart wheel slamming it to an abrupt halt against the Peepal tree. The driver came rolling down and slammed himself against the upturned vehicle. He looked up stunned at the remains of the vehicle above him. The vehicle looked as though it was standing on its head with the front harness of the cart at the base of the tree and the rear end propped against the tree trunk. The bullocks were nowhere to be seen as they had rolled down the hill.

The bullock cart driver had taken a terrific beating on his way down and was badly bruised. He had been stunned into inactivity as he looked at the hillside above him. He did not know that T20 had started his downward journey.

T20 was surprised at the way the bullock cart had disappeared down the hill. He walked to the edge of the road and peered down. Birds and monkeys were creating a ruckus. In the distance he saw the rear end of the cart propped against the Peepal tree so he entered the bushes and started his careful down hill climb. He hopped over little bushes and other obstacles, roared and loped down. The forest was alive with all sorts of sounds and noises. A multitude of scared birds had taken to the air and were flying in circles above the area of the accident. They made a din as they flew around yelling their warning to the forest. Monkeys chattered and jumped excitedly from branch to branch as snakes slithered away. Their privacy had been shattered when the cart crashed past them. Insects and little animals were scampering off to be far away from the accident.

T20 loped down the hill in the direction of the upturned cart. He crashed through shrubs and bushes disturbing a myriad of creatures that lived in the undergrowth. He burst out from some bushes and stopped. Twenty feet below him was the upturned cart propped against the tree.

The tiger snarled. The stricken bullock cart driver heard the snarl and snapped back to his senses. He looked up, screamed, and dived past the upturned cart. He rolled down the hillside and like an animal he loped on all fours till he finally was on his legs and running down the hill. The tiger roared and loped after him. It was soon near enough to pounce on the man. It sprang and landed on the running mans back. The man was thrown forward causing him to cart wheel, somersault, and roll down the hill with the tiger loping down beside him. The man hit some bushes and stopped. The tiger slammed its forepaws on the ground to stop but skidded instead. The momentum of his heavy body caused him to crash through some bushes and stop ten feet below the human.

The bullock cart driver screamed and scrambled up hill on the route he had rolled down. The Peepal tree with the propped cart was forty feet above him. The tiger gathered itself, roared, lunged forward and loped up. It loped through the bushes it had crashed through and saw the bullock cart driver scramble up. The bullocks were nowhere to be seen. They had rolled down and were lying and belching at the base of the hill.

The tiger loped up and grabbed the bullock cart driver's feet in its mouth and dragged him down.

"Aaaaaaargh, help," the bullock cart driver screamed as he tried his best to drag himself and the feet holding tiger up. The tiger dragged him screaming down the hill.

"Help," yelled the driver. "Help, please someone help me."

The tiger stopped pulling and let go of the leg. He strode over the stricken man's body and straddled him. The man screamed and pushed the head away with his bare hands. A slap from the tigers paw silenced him.

T20 looked down at his victim, lowered his head, took the neck in his mouth and dragged the unconscious man further down the hill.

Chapter(10) One more night over a kill

The Jeep roared down the forest road as it meandered along the rutted dirt track kicking up dust behind it as it roared on. It was the forest departments Ford Jeep which Henry Phibb's loved riding. He felt one with the old American vehicle. He and the Jeep were both elderly Americans who had made India their home.

The Jeep roared on as Ram Singh steered it along the forest track. The vehicle did a sort of jig over the uneven road shaking Henry's old bones causing him to grimace. The vehicle sometimes skipped and bounced as the old leaf springs in the vehicles ancient suspension winced at the beating they received from the road. Phibb's tried to have a conversation with Ram Singh over the roar of the Jeeps old petrol engine. Ram Singh concentrated on driving the vehicle.

The Jeep soon reached the spot where the bullocks had panicked and dragged the bullock cart off the road. A crowd of bare backed villagers were standing on the edge of the road and were peering down. The Jeep drew up and braked. Ram Singh and Henry climbed off the vehicle. Henry took his rifle which was lying on the front seat and the two men walked up to the villagers.

"Sir, look down there," a tall turbaned man said. "The bullock cart is propped against that tree."

Henry and Ram Singh peered down. Sure enough, two hundred feet down was the upturned bullock cart propped against the Peepal tree. It seemed as though it was in some yogic pose and was standing on its head with the tree as a support. Henry walked carefully down closely followed by Ram Singh.

"It seems the tiger attacked the bullock cart on the road," Henry told Ram Singh as the two carefully walked down. "The bullocks must have panicked and run off the road."

Ram Singh nodded his head as he negotiated his way down the hill stepping gingerly between shrubs and bushes as he followed Henry. The two walked past bags of rice and rice strewn on the hillside where the bags had burst open. They reached the Peepal tree and looked at the upturned bullock cart.

"It must have been one hell of a roll over when the cart came down this hill," Henry said.

"Yes sir, it must have been horrible," Ram Singh replied. "With the cart and rice bags rolling down the hill, I think some of the rice has been stolen."

Henry shrugged. He knew the people living in the villages which pock marked the forest were extremely poor and weren't averse to pilfering to make ends meet. Anyway that was none of his business. It was the job of the police to investigate what happened to the rice. "When did this take place?" he asked.

"No one knows," Ram Singh replied. "People only say that the rice distributor was missing for the last three days. A cow herd that was grazing his cows in this area discovered the upturned cart yesterday. They don't know whether the rice distributor is alive or dead. All they know is that he hasn't been distributing rice for the last three days. They assume he may have been killed and eaten by the tiger."

Henry shrugged as he peered down the hillside. The foliage was disturbed below him and in places it had been flattened. The flattened foliage told Henry that some sort of struggle did take place here. The greenery could have been flattened or may not have been flattened by the rice distributor. But the bullocks must have certainly rolled down the steep gradient.

"Let's go down and investigate," Henry said.

Ram Singh nodded his head in agreement so the two men walked down followed by two villagers to the spot where the foliage was flattened. Henry sat down on his knees and studied the flattened patch. There were drops of blood.

"He killed the man here," Henry said.

Ram Singh nodded his head.

"Let's go down lower. Let's see what we can find," Henry suggested.

The two men and the two villagers walked down and reached the base of the hill. Sure enough, two buffalo's lay dead partly hidden by clumps of bushes. A dozen vultures and two hyenas were feeding on the carcass which had an army of flies buzzing over it. The hyena's giggled as they greedily gouged into the carcass. Ram Sing picked up a stone and shouted at the scavengers as he threw the stone at them. The vultures hopped away and some of them took to the air. The hyena's simply slunk away. Another stone from Ram Singh sent the remaining vultures flapping into the air to simply perch themselves on trees above the kill from where they looked with distaste at the approaching humans. The humans covered their nose to ward off the stench as they studied the carcass. Henry walked past the carcass followed by Ram Singh and the two villagers and reached the stream the tiger had slaked its thirst in. They could make out the drag marks on the ground on the other side of the stream so they entered the stream and waded in the cold water till they reached the other side. Their drenched shoes made loud squelching sounds as they walked towards the flattened grass. They realized they were in a valley between two hills. The drag marks on the thick grass continued up the hill so now if they wanted to continue tracking the kill they would have to trek uphill. The two decided to continue so they walked slowly and carefully up the hill. They walked under the canopy of a huge banyan tree. They walked past the tree and climbed two hundred feet up when they saw flies buzzing over some bushes.

Henry carefully approached the bush. He shoved his left hand into his trouser pocket and pulled out his handkerchief. He covered his nose with it while Ram Singh did the same. The stench was overpowering. The mangled remains of the rice distributor lay in the bushes.

Ram Singh once more sat on his haunches and vomited.

"Ram Singh, you're a sissy," Henry said. "I'm ashamed of you. Now bring yourself together and behave like a man. You are a forest officer. You should be used to seeing these things. You will experience many ghastly things during your stint as an officer. So buck up and be bold."

Ram Singh continued vomiting.

"If you keep vomiting every time we see a dead body, how will you be of use to me? We have work to do tonight. This tiger has made it a habit of making us sit over a kill and never returning to it," Henry said.

One of the villagers who had accompanied the two down the hill was asked to go back and fetch a chachri from his village. This was done and the bamboo platform was placed on two adjacent branches of two Jamun trees twelve feet above the ground. Henry climbed onto the platform and was soon asleep. Ram Singh kept a vigil all through the night. He saw some deer pass by, sat awake absorbing the forests night sounds, saw a wild pig snort and walk past right under his tree, watched fireflies and glow worms all through the night. But there was no tiger. Ram Singh was glad when twilight peeped through the forest cover. He woke Henry up and the two climbed down the tree.

"Sahib, Now what do we do? This tiger is roaming in this forest killing people left right and center, and never returns to the kill. It has made us run a weird gauntlet forcing us to sit the whole night with dead putrid smelling mutilated bodies. Now what do we do sir."

"Start a beat," Henry said.

"What's a beat?"

"Good god, don't you know what a beat is?"

Ram Singh was embarrassed. "No sahib, I don't know what a beat is," he said.

"A beat involves more than a hundred men. They fan out across a certain section of the jungle and beat drums, tin cans, anything that makes a lot of noise. That includes fire crackers. The beaters beat the bush and walk towards the hunter who is waiting in ambush. This is an easy way to flush out an animal and kill it, especially if it is as elusive as our friend T20. The British invented this method of hunting. This method helped them slaughter animals in the hundreds. And they called the dead animal's trophies."

Ram Singh stared at Henry. "So I will have to assemble a hundred able bodied men for the beat?" he asked.

"Yes, but the number is five hundred to be precise."

Ram Singh was incredulous. "How am I supposed to get so many men? And from where? The forest department only employs twelve of us."

Phibb's stared at Ram Singh. "Young man, how did you get your job? I have a suspicion you bribed yourself into the forest service."

"I sat for the public service commission and competed," Ram Singh replied indignantly. "I have less knowledge than you because times have changed. Today's forest department officers are deliberately not taught how to hunt or to capture animals like in your time. This is the age of forest conservation."

"And what sort of training did you get?"

Ram Singh smiled. "The trainer was absent most of the time. Moreover, the beat you are talking about is done to capture or kill animals. Today's forest department officials aren't trained to capture and kill animals. The main focus of our job is forest conservation and animal protection. Not animal slaughter. The beat you talk about is a thing of the past. It is history, a sort of fairy tale for us."

Henry smiled. "You've got a point there," he said. "I've grown old. I think I am a thing of the past, a remnant of a bygone era. I am a black and white photograph amongst colored ones. I accept it. I do harbor some outdated ideas."

Ram Singh smiled. "Sir, I am tired. Let's go and relax in the forest bungalow. I will ask my fellow officers to arrange for five hundred people for the beat."

Henry nodded his head and the two waded across the stream and climbed up the slope past the upturned bullock cart to the road on top of the hill and the waiting Jeep. Henry climbed into the passenger seat while Ram Singh climbed into the seat behind the steering wheel. He switched on the vehicles ignition and swung the steering wheel in a full circle turning the Jeep around. He drove the Jeep back to the forest bungalow where Henry had a nice hot water bath in the bungalows hot water swimming pool as the forest department cook prepared breakfast for the two. Ram Singh was in a hurry so he did not wait for his breakfast as he had work to do. He went to the forest office in Jamui town to get help to arrange five hundred beaters for tomorrows beat.

Henry sat relaxed in the hot water pool as the sulfur water took away the uncomfortable feeling in his body which was due to sleeping the whole night on a bamboo chachri. He lolled in the water for an hour, got up, took a towel which a turbaned servant was holding and wiped his body. He retired to his room to enjoy a sumptuous breakfast of eggs, toast, a glass of milk, and wild honey stolen from the forests bees. After breakfast he would prepare himself for tomorrows beat.

Chapter(11) The beat

There was excitement in the grounds of the forest department bungalow. Today was the day of the beat. Henry was sitting on the bungalow's porch sipping a beer. Ram Singh had gone the other day to the office of the forest department in Jamui and gathered the staff. They climbed into Jeeps or onto waiting motorcycles and headed for the Bhim Bandh forest bungalow to take a briefing from Henry on what to do. Henry briefed them and sent them into the forest to fan out in the different villages and bring the headman of each village nestled in the forest to the bungalow. By evening around thirty five headmen were assembled in front of the bungalow's porch to hear what Henry had to say. His strategy was simple. Each headman would bring ten able bodied men from his village armed with spears and knives for self defense. They would bring along drums, or tin cans, and sticks to beat the drums and tin cans with. A hill would be chosen to the left of the Bhim Bandh hot spring where people would fan out and surround the hill. Henry, Ram Singh and a couple of armed forest officers would position themselves on a tree near the base of the hill to the right of the hot water springs. They would wait in ambush as the beaters who were positioned to the left of the hot springs beat their way across the jungle to the right towards the people sitting in ambush. They prayed to god that the tiger was flushed out of the jungle. They would repeat the flushing process on hill after hill so that most of Bhim Bandh forest area was flushed. They would gun down the tiger if it attempted to escape. They had already flushed two hills but with no result. A myriad of birds were disturbed. Two sloth bears, a dozen deer, and some wild dogs had run for their lives. But there was no tiger so, the group had taken an interval giving the villagers who were doing the flushing a breather allowing them to have their lunch. Ram Singh and Henry drove back to the bungalow for their meal.

Ram Singh emerged from his room and looked at Henry. "Are you ready sir," he asked.

"As ready as father Freddy," Henry replied with a smile.

"Then should we go? The beaters have had their lunch and are waiting for us. There will be one more beat today. We will have to finish it before nightfall."

Henry Phibb's stood up, picked up his rifle which was lying on the table, and walked with Ram Singh to the Jeep. They climbed into their respective seats and Ram Singh switched on the old American's ignition. The engine coughed, sputtered, and roared to life to the relief of its occupants. They were always on tenterhooks on whether it would start or not. It was a rejected vehicle, but Phibb's insisted on using it.

Ram Singh let go of the clutch and the vehicle roared toward the forest department compounds gates. It roared out of the gate and turned right to travel down the rutted dirt track. Ram Singh drove fast as six hundred men were waiting for the two on the hill called Nakul Parbat. They were eager to continue the hunt. Everyone wanted to see the man eating tiger dead.

"Henry sir," Ram Singh said as he drove.

"Yes."

"I was wondering how I would manage to gather five hundred able bodied men for the beat. We have employed five hundred men for the whole day and will have to give them at least a day's wages. The forest department does not have money to sustain more beats. It has cost the department at least one hundred thousand rupees for just a day's flushing of the forest. This is too expensive. If we don't bag the tiger today politicians will ask questions. We will be in trouble."

Henry smiled. I knew they wouldn't do it for free. But I knew they would agree to do it. It's in their own interest. The tiger has hampered their freedom of movement in the forest. Each and every villager wants to see the tiger dead. That is why they are helping out and that is why I asked you to bring five hundred able bodied men."

"So you knew all along the villagers would jump and accept the chance in helping to get rid of the man eater."

Henry nodded his head and looked ahead at the road in front of the madly bucking Jeep. He looked behind him and could only see the dust the vehicles rear wheels were kicking up. "The villagers living in the vicinity of the beat always did it for free," he said. "During British colonial rule the beaters got a share of the kill to feast on. Animals were killed in the hundreds in a single hunt. The meat was divided equally amongst the beaters."

Ram Singh listened to Henry as he looked ahead at the road before him along which he was steering the Jeep. "Sir, it's a pity we aren't allowed to shoot animals for game. We are part of the world's forest preservation campaign. Otherwise I would have loved to borrow your rifle and take a shot at a deer. There were so many animals trying to escape the beaters, I felt like simply hopping off our tree and catching one. It seemed so easy."

Henry laughed.

"I wanted you to shoot a deer for dinner. But I know you don't believe in breaking rules. So I didn't suggest it," Ram Singh said.

"Yes, it is your job to follow rules. You are a forest officer and you have to set an example."

The Jeep roared on and soon reached the base of the hill called Nakul Parbat. Ram Singh braked and stopped at the side of the road leaving enough space for a vehicle to pass through. Four bare bodied dhoti clad turbaned men were waiting for them.

"Are we late?" Ram Singh asked as he climbed off the Jeep.

"No sahib," a villager said who had his hands folded in a Namaste to the officer and the American. "The beaters have just had their food. They have positioned themselves around the hill and are resting. They are waiting to start the beat."

Henry stepped out of the Jeep and walked to the edge of the road. "Okay, the signal will be my rifle shot," he said. "As soon as I fire my rifle the beaters will start the beat. They will move down the hill in such a manner that the animals being flushed out of the forest are forced to ford the stream under the Peepal tree on whose branch I will be sitting and waiting. And no one must hide themselves. Make as much noise as possible. Everyone has had his lunch so the lungs should have extra energy. Shout and scream for all you are worth and bang the drums and tin cans as loudly as possible. The ruckus you make should be so loud that astronauts in outer space should hear it."

Ram Singh was the only person who understood the joke. He laughed as the villagers turned and disappeared into the jungle. Henry and Ram Singh left the road and walked into the jungle foliage slowly pushing their way down through the greenery."

"I hope the tiger is flushed out in this beat," Ram Singh said. "The beaters are poor people. They have to eke out a living by foraging daily in the forest. The forest department does not have money to pay five hundred people two days labor. If the tiger isn't flushed out we will have to wait a week to afford a beat again. And in that one week a couple of more humans may lose their lives. And what guarantee is there that the tiger will be flushed out in the next beat."

"There's no guarantee," Henry replied. "We'll just have to keep on trying."

The two walked down the hillside and at the base of the hill they broke out of forest cover. There was a two hundred feet broad valley before them with a forest stream traveling through the middle. A group of black buck, wild boar, half a dozen piglets and some storks were disturbed. The storks were wading in the streams shallow water pecking at the water in futile attempts to catch little fish that darted around. The black buck and wild pigs were either grazing on the fauna on the streams banks or slaking their thirst in the stream. Seeing the human intrusion into their privacy, the storks flapped their wings and flew off perching themselves on trees that were one hundred feet up the opposite hill. Black buck ran across the stream, across the open plot of land, up the hillside on the opposite side to finally disappear like ghosts in the greenery.

"It's a pity we disturbed them," Henry said. "I used to visit this place regularly when I was in service. It's a garden of Eden down here."

The two walked down to the base of the hill and waded into the stream. The water was cold but felt nice in the feet. They didn't mind their keds getting wet. They waded out of the stream on the opposite side and walked across the patch of grassy land over which the black buck had run. They reached the base of the hill on the opposite side and walked across the plot of land and started the climb up. They walked slowly for Henry's sake.

The two climbed the hillside for a hundred feet and entered the thick jungle foliage. They brushed ferns, twigs, branches and leaves as they walked up. They heard the lonely 'Kwa-aakwa-aa-kwa-aa' of a peacock in the jungle above them on the hillside. The 'kwa-aa-kwa-aa' was picked up by other 'kwa-aa-kwa-aa's' as other peacocks picked up the call and informed the jungle about the human intrusion.

"The peacock has given us away," Ram Singh said as he panted up the hill.

"The jungle does have an interesting warning system," Henry said as he labored up the hill behind Ram Singh. He was also panting heavily. The two reached the Peepal tree on which a platform had been built by connecting two branches with wooden planks hammered to them. The forest department had been gracious enough to supply Ram Singh with wooden planks, a hammer, and three dozen nails."

"That looks comfortable," Henry said as he walked up to the tree and looked up. Ram Singh walked up to him and looked up to admire his own work.

"Did I do a nice job sir?" Ram Singh asked.

"You certainly did. Here hold my rifle while I climb up."

Ram Singh extended his right hand and took hold of the rifle. Henry then grappled up the tree. He reached the wooden platform and hauled himself onto it after which he lay on his stomach on the platform and extended his hand down for his rifle. "Send the rifle up," he said.

Ram Singh took the rifle by the butt and sent the barrel up towards Henry. The latter took hold of the barrel and pulled the weapon up. He sat up, fished out the magazine from his trouser pocket and shoved it into the slot in the stock. He pulled back the bolt and let a brass colored bullet hop into the breach. He pushed back the bolt and released the safety catch. He looked at Ram Singh as the latter hauled himself onto the platform and sat cross legged next to Henry.

"Give the signal sir," Ram Singh said.

"Okay, let the hunt begin," Henry said as he put the rifle's butt to his shoulder, pointed the barrel skywards and fired. The crack was ear splitting but was instantly answered by shouting and yelling from the top of the hill in front of them. Hundreds of people beat drums and tin cans and yelled at the top of their voices as they started their slow accent downhill screaming and shouting to scare the animals into running in the direction of the hunters in the tree.

Henry smiled and waited while an eager Ram Singh scanned the hillside before him. They had a bird's eye view of a whole kilometer of the valley through which the forest stream flowed.

"Keep your fingers crossed Ram Singh," Henry said.

"I have my fingers crossed sir," Ram Singh replied.

Henry concentrated his gaze on the open land on the section of the valley which was on the opposite side of the stream which was directly below the forest line. He scanned it for animals that were running away from the din.

"You look to the left," Henry ordered Ram Singh. "While I concentrate on the right."

Ram Singh did as he was ordered to do and concentrated on the left side of the valley below the forest line.

"Whisper if you see a tiger," Henry whispered.

Henry watched intently with his gaze fixed on the forest line. A bunch of chital deer appeared from the forest and ran down the slope to the valley. They ran across the valley, thrashed water into spray as the waded and galloped across the stream to the side where the hunters were sitting. They galloped to the base of the hill and galloped up the hillside to finally fade into the tree line.

"Sir, I wish I lived in the British colonial days," Ram Singh whispered. "It would have been an experience shooting those deer that came out in the open."

A wild boar grunted and walked out from under the tree line directly in front of Henry. It wobbled down the slope, stopped, grunted, and ran towards the stream. It crossed the stream just as a sow with twelve piglets emerged from under the tree line. The sow grunted and ran down the hill to the valley closely followed by the squealing piglets. The pig family crossed the stream, turned downstream, and ran on disappearing behind some boulders.

Ram Singh was staring to the left and saw a couple of huge antlered Bara Singha's emerging from the forest. They galloped down to the stream, turned downstream and galloped away. "Now I understand how the British managed to kill so many animals in the hunts. I've seen old black and white pictures of old British hunting expeditions. I never understood how they managed to kill so many animals in a single hunt. It's so simple. We don't have to do anything. Simply aim, shoot, and kill, and count the trophies. Those hunts were unfair to the animals."

"Yes," Henry said as he concentrated on the valley to the right. 'The beat ended in slaughter. It was unfair."

The two listened for fifteen minutes to the din the beaters were making. They heard a roar. Ram Singhs hair stood on end. The roar came again reverberating through the valley. Henry tightened his grip on the rifles stock as his right hand for finger curled around the trigger. He scanned the valley before him. He had grown tense. It was a long time since he had last killed a living thing and the tiger he was supposed to kill was his own baby. He had watched T20 and T19 grow up since they were cubs into full fledged tigers. He had watched them hunt and kill prey in the river several times. He was now supposed to kill one of them. It was though he was sitting in ambush to kill his own child.

A couple of sambars galloped out from under the tree line. They galloped across the valley and thrashed the water of the stream as they galloped across it. While the sambars were mid stream, the tigers roar echoed once again in the forest. This caused the beaters to increase the din they were making and gave the sambars the impetus to gallop faster. They soon disappeared into the jungle on Henry's side.

"Sir, the tiger is coming down the hillside. I thought I saw something yellow crash through the foliage up there," Ram Singh said as he pointed at the hillside five hundred feet up.

"Are you sure it was the tiger?" Henry asked.

"I'm not sure. It was a yellow flash in the madly rustling foliage."

"Keep an eye on it and inform me immediately as soon as it emerges from under the tree line. I'll keep a vigil on this side."

Some more deer ran out from under the tree line. They ran down into the valley, crossed the stream, ran across the stream to Henry's side of the valley, ran up the incline on Henry's side and disappeared into the jungle."

The roar was heard again and the tiger emerged from under the tree line.

Ram Singh was excited as he was scared and tense. He was experiencing mixed feelings as he grabbed Henry's arm and shook it. "Sir, the tiger is there."

Henry turned his head to look in the direction Ram Singh was pointing. Sure enough a tiger was walking down the hillside slope. Henry brought his rifle around, put the butt against his shoulder, curled his right hand for finger around the trigger and aimed the rifle at the tiger. He shut his left eye peering through his right eye down the rifle sight at the tiger. The rifle sight was properly aligned with the tiger which was walking downhill. Henry let the barrel follow the tiger. Ram Singh had both his fore fingers pressed into his ears and braced himself for the rifle crack and the action which could follow. Ram Singh watched as the tiger walked to the forest spring expecting to hear the rifle shot any moment. The rifle crack did not come so Ram Singh turned his head towards Henry. He was surprised to see that Henry had lowered his rifle and was peering at the tiger.

"What happened sir, why aren't you aiming the rifle at the tiger?"

Henry kept his eyes glued on the animal as it waded across the stream as he replied. "That isn't a tiger. It is a tigress. I know her. She's T19."

"Are you sure?"

"As sure as someone could possibly be. I watched those tigers since their birth. That's T19, it's not T20."

The tigress crossed the stream, loped across the valley, loped up the hill and disappeared into the forest. The two waited and soon the beaters showed themselves on the hill above. They continued shouting and beating drums and tin cans making a din as they beat their way down. It took them a full twenty minutes to come down. It was a unique scene. Approximately six hundred beaters emerged from under the tree line and marched down the hill to the valley below. Most of them were tired so when they reached the banks of the stream they put down their drums and tin cans and slumped down to the ground for a rest. Some slurped up palms full of stream water to quench their thirst and cool their bodies.

"Here hold this rifle while I climb down," Henry said as he put the rifle on Ram Singh's lap. He climbed down the tree, stood on the ground, and lifted his arm for the rifle. Ram Singh took the rifle by the barrel and lowered the butt down. Henry took hold of the butt end of the rifle and took hold of the weapon after which he turned to face a group of villagers who had walked up the hill to where he was standing. They walked up to him and folded their hands to him in a Namaste. Henry folded his hands and wished them back.

"Sahib," a villager said. "Why didn't you shoot the tiger?"

"Because it wasn't the man eating tiger. it was the tigress."

Ram Singh clambered down the tree.

"But it was the tiger," a villager said.

Henry looked at Ram Singh and then turned his gaze back to the villagers. "The man eater is not a tigress. It is a male. It's name is T20. I think you all know that. I aimed at the animal but realized my mistake. I recognized the tigress. It was T19."

Ram Singh and the villagers walked down the slope with Henry.

"That means today's beat was also a failure," Ram Singh asked.

The little group reached the base of the hill.

"Where could T20 be?" Ram Singh wondered.

"I don't know, but where ever he is we have to find him and kill him and capture him."

The group of humans waded through the stream and crossed to the other side.

Chapter(12) Midnight kill

Sher Singh was a wood cutter. He was well to do in his village because of his habit of illegally chopping down trees and smuggling the wood out of the forest to sell it in the town of Jamui. He lived in a shack in the middle of the village that went by the name of Bidupur. His house boasted of a cot, a table, two chairs, and his wife cooked food on a kerosene stove. He got his regular supply of kerosene from the nearby town.

Today was an ordinary day just like the other days. He would go into the forest, chop a tree down, smuggle the wood out of the forest and sell it in the market in the town of Jamui. That is why he was having his bath in the hand pump he had drilled in the ground behind his shack. He sat cross legged on the ground in front of a bucket of water and dunked mugs of water over himself.

Sher Singh was well built. He was chocolate brown in complexion, six feet tall, with broad shoulders and bulging muscles on his arms. His daily job of chopping wood had built those muscles. He dunked the last mug of water over himself, stood up, and picked up a towel that was lying on the ground nearby. It was on top of his dhoti. Sher Singh wiped his body with the towel and strung it on a rope that was tied to his shack and a Peepal tree. He picked up the dhoti and wrapped it around himself with one end going between his thighs to finally tuck it in the back. He was bare foot because he never wore shoes.

Sher Singh entered the shack and realized his wife was cooking food on the kerosene stove. "How long will it take for food to be prepared?" he asked.

"It will take half an hour at least."

Sher Singh turned to face the idol of the Hindu god Rama which stood in the north western corner of the shack on a chair. He mumbled a silent prayer, bent down, and picked up an axe and some rope. Holding the axe over his shoulder, he walked out of the shack and remembered something. He had forgotten to take the little mirror along with him. Henry Phibb's and Ram Singh had visited the village and told the villagers about the tiger and advised them on how to protect themselves from the animal. The wood cutter had taken the advice seriously and always carried a little mirror tucked away in his dhoti when he roamed the forest. When he chose a tree he wanted to chop down, he would hang the mirror on the tree right in front of him while he proceeded to chop the base of the tree with his eyes periodically glancing at the mirror. The wood cutter was no fool. The sound of him chopping wood disturbed the peace in the jungle. The noise was too loud and reverberated through the jungle. Either the noise scared animals away, or it would attract a hungry animal who wouldn't mind devouring a human, and the last thing the wood cutter wanted, was to land up as chewed meat in a man eating tigers belly. This is why he always took the mirror along with him. It helped him keep an eye on the area behind him while he chopped wood.

The wood cutter turned around and walked back into his shack. The mirror was lying on his wooden cot so he picked it up, tucked it in his dhoti and walked out. He walked down the single rutted street, entered the jungle and left the village behind. He followed a narrow path through the forest and felt free outside the village as though he was out of a prison. The village was his prison, the forest his freedom. He enjoyed the forests sounds. He enjoyed the chirps, squawks, and songs of different birds, the buzz of insects, and the rustle of leaves in the wind. This was oxygen, pure oxygen, and not the adulterated polluted air he breathed in the town of Jamui.

There was a time when the wood cutter would enjoy a relaxed walk in this paradise which he called his home. He would spot wild animals and scamper up into the safety of a tree. It wasn't that he was frightened of the animal. He knew the laws of nature and had simply saved himself. Neither did he panic when he would spot a sloth bear half way up a tree. He knew it wouldn't disturb him if he didn't disturb it. That's why he would refuse to chop wood in an area where he spotted a sloth bear. He did not want to irritate it or disturb it. But today was different. The man eating tiger had created havoc in and around the villages of Bhim Bandh. It had killed and devoured more than five dozen humans. Some of the victims were well built wood cutters like himself. Unfortunately well built men were no match for a man eating tiger.

The wood cutter inhaled in deeply as he walked on. He disturbed a pair of doves who were courting each other. "Shoo," he yelled and watched the doves fly off. He continued walking and disturbed a peahen. She yelled a surprised "kwa-aaa," and dashed off to the right disappearing into the jungle. The wood cutter walked on and soon reached the tree he wanted to chop. It was a teak tree eight inches in diameter at the base tapering to three inches at the top. The broad green leaves helped in creating a canopy that provided shade to the ground. Teak wood was expensive and was used in making furniture and frames for doors and windows. This tree would allow him to bring home some extra money today. So he put his axe and rope on the ground, fished out the mirror from the folds of his dhoti and hung it in a groove in the bark of the tree in level with his chest. He picked up his axe, glanced at the mirror, and swung the axe down. The sharp end of the axe hit the wood, slicing half an inch going right through the bark and getting stuck in the wood. The wood cutter pulled hard and wrenched the axe out, lifted it above his head and swung it down sideways against the wood. His aim was perfect and the sharp end of the axe hit the slit in the wood which it had previously made. The axe went in deeper by a quarter of a millimeter. The grass cutter wrenched the axe out of the wood and looked at the mirror. He did not know that his act of faithfully glancing at the mirror would save his life.

Unknown to the grass cutter when he left the village, T20 had been sitting two hundred feet up on the slope of the hill that was directly behind the village. It had been stalking the village for the last three hours and was now studying the village and the villagers and planning to make a kill. It was on the verge of getting up and slinking down to the village when it noticed the grass cutter walk out of the shack, walk out of the village and enter the jungle. That was exactly what T20 was searching for, a lone target. He had been successfully driven out from several villages quite a few times and realized it could be dangerous trying to kill a human inside a village. He now concentrated on soft targets, lone humans in the jungle. And the grass cutter was a lone human going alone into the jungle.

T20 made sure he was hidden properly as he quietly stood up and slunk down the hillside. A monkey spotted him and chattered a warning to the jungle. A peacock recognized the cause for the monkeys chatter and picked up the call and yelled out its own "kwa-aa's-kwa-aa's" to the jungle. The tiger was unperturbed at being spotted as it thought that humans did not understand Jungle noises. He quietly slunk through the undergrowth behind the village. He walked soundlessly with the help of his padded feet and soon left the village behind. The tiger turned right and walked towards the path the grass cutter had taken. Reaching the path, it turned north and followed the path in its desire to stalk the grass cutter. A couple of monkeys that were eating on a wild jamun tree saw him and chattered their irritation at him, showing him their teeth. Unperturbed T20 walked on.

The grass cutter continued chopping the tree as he occasionally glanced into the mirror in front of him. T20 walked down the path and heard the chops so he slunk to his left and hid under some ferns. After a minute he slunk out and walked soundlessly towards where the chopping was taking place. He slunk on keeping himself concealed under trees and through bushes and at last saw the grass cutter as the latter continued chopping at the wood.

T20 peered at the grass cutter through the ferns. The latter stopped, wiped the perspiration from his face, and stood for a moment giving his tired muscles a chance to relax.

T20 stared at the grass cutter and watched as the person once more picked up the axe, swung it over his shoulder, and swung it down at the base of the tree. This was the best time to attack the grass cutter. The human was concentrating on the tree and was oblivious of what was going on behind him. That was what the tiger thought as it slunk slowly out of the underbrush. Paw after slow soundless paw T20 slunk forward.

The grass cutter continued chopping wood. He had hacked halfway into trunk and needed to hack just two inches more to be able to finally push the tree down.

The wood cutter wrenched the axe out of the wood, lifted the iron end above his right shoulder, glanced at the mirror and noticed the ochre and white discoloring in the foliage. But the rhythm of swinging the axe down caused him to swing the axe down into the wood. In that fraction of a second while he wrenched the axe out of the wood he realized the ochre and white discoloring in the foliage forty feet behind him was the man eating tiger. He pretended he did not see the tiger and lifted the axe above his shoulder and glanced at the mirror. Yes, it was the tiger and it was slowly creeping forward hunched low towards him.

The grass cutter froze. "Don't be scared," he said to himself as he stood waiting with his axe above his shoulder as he stared into the mirror. He watched the crouched tiger creep towards him. A shiver went down his spine. He felt extremely vulnerable alone here in the jungle with the man eating tiger stalking him. "Don't be scared, be cool, remain calm, or you will die," he told himself.

The tiger crept forward and failed to notice the human had stopped chopping wood. It did not strike him that the human, for some unknown reason, was standing motionless. It simply accepted the fact that the humans back was towards him and this was a perfect time to attack.

The wood cutter perspired as he stared at the tiger silently creeping up at him in the mirror. He let the animal creep up to a spot which was fifteen feet behind him. His unblinking eyes watched it come closer. And then he saw it crouched in what he thought would be a spring. The tiger sprang and the wood cutter swiveled around on his heels swinging the axe with all his might. He realized he was too fast as he missed. The mirror was a concave mirror which showed the tiger to be closer than where it actually was. This caused the grass cutter to miscalculate and start his swing a fraction of a second too early. He had aimed at the tigers face but missed it because it wasn't there. The tiger however had sprung and was air born as the wood cutter realized his mistake and without stopping his swing, he bent low and continued swiveling around, this time in a second circle to attempt a second shot which, having seen the tiger, he knew wouldn't miss. He was still bent low as his axe connected beautifully into the tiger's shoulder blade, chipping it and glancing off the shoulder blade to hit the face, flicking the tiger's body of course to the left thereby missing him. The tiger was blinded by the hit as it saw red and saw stars as it roared in pain. It landed on the ground and loped off.

The terrified wood cutter stood up and ran to a nearby wood apple tree and clambered up it to a branch fifteen above the ground. He could hear the tiger's angry roars in the distance. It was a close shave with death and the wood cutter felt safe in the thorny tree. He shivered when he heard a couple of painful 'aouns' in the distance.

The wood cutter remained in the tree for three whole hours. He didn't have the courage to come down again. He knew he had injured the tiger. And an injured tiger was an angry tiger which was dangerous. The worst part was that he didn't know where it was? That is why he remained perched in the tree. He was in a fix. He would have to climb down if he was to go back to the safety of his village. He was delighted and thanked his luck when he heard humans. Half a dozen villagers walked into view. They were all bare backed people who had gone into the jungle to collect Tendu leaves to sell in the market. That is why each man was carrying a stack of leaves each. They were the wood cutters friends and would accompany him to Jamui town to sell the leaves to manufacturers who made Tendu leaf plates with the leaves.

"Pssssssssssssssst," pssssssss'ed the wood cutter as the people walked past him. They were his co villagers and were going back to the village.

The Tendu leaf collectors stopped, looked up, and recognized the wood cutter. The latter was waving to them making a sign for them to come up.

"The man eating tiger is somewhere around," the wood cutter said from his perch. "It chased me up this tree."

This alarmed the people who were standing below the tree. They looked around. "There is no tiger around," said a tall bare backed man.

"Come down, there is no tiger around," said another bare backed man. "Come with us back to the village."

The wood cutter grappled down the tree, hopped onto the ground, picked up his axe and rope and followed the men on their way back to the village. He was lucky the men were passing by. He now at least had company to the village.

Entering the village, the villagers dispersed and disappeared into their mud huts. The wood cutter entered his hut, put his axe down on the mud floor, and lay down on his cot. He was trembling. He had a narrow escape today. It would be quite some time before he could gather enough courage to enter the forest to cut wood again. He would have to enjoy a forced holiday on himself.

The wood cutter waited patiently for his wife to come back from where ever she had gone. It was evening by the time she showed herself at her door. She had gone visiting some women who lived six huts away from hers. The wood cutter told her his harrowing story and how he narrowly escaped the tiger. Henry Phibb's short speech, on how to protect oneself in case a tiger attacked, saved his life. He was grateful to the white American sahib for taking the pains to come to his remote village and tell them how to protect themselves.

The wood cutters wife cooked food as the evening drew on and darkness took over the forest. There was no electricity in the village so the wood cutter lit a kerosene lantern and sat cross legged on the cot waiting for his food. His wife ladled a plateful of potato curry into a steel plate and handed it to him. He put the plate on the cot in front of himself. She then handed five baked neatly wrapped chapattis to him. The wood cutter took the chapatti's and tore out pieces, dipped the pieces in gravy and proceeded to eat. He ate his fill and handed the empty plate to his wife, walked out of the back of the hut to his hand pump, pumped some water and washed his hands. He walked back into the shack and lay down. It was time to go to sleep.

The wood cutters wife carried the utensils to the hand pump, put them down below the pumps spout, pumped water on them, washed the utensils and carried them back into the hut where she placed them in a corner. She then blew out the lantern allowing the hut to be plunged into darkness after which she laid her tired body on the cot beside her sleeping husband and closed her eyes to go to sleep. As the couple slept they were oblivious to the fact that T20 was having another attempt at killing a human being. The tiger was hungry and though he had been slightly injured from the blow from the wood cutters axe, he was going to attempt again at midnight.

T20 had received the blow and loped off. It was confused and in great pain. And it was hungry. That is why it turned around and loped to the spot it was hiding in the afternoon on the slope of the hill behind the village where it sat and licked its wound. It peered down at the village through the ferns as evening drew away and darkness overtook the jungle. At around midnight it ventured down the hill and headed towards an alley between two huts. It walked silently with the help of its padded feet and stopped at the mouth of the alley where it sniffed the air. It stood crouched low for a minute and entered the alley.

T20 was in the dark and couldn't be seen. He walked up the alley and walked past mud hut after mud hut till it reached the single street that travelled through the village. A dog was lying twenty feet down the road. It suddenly cocked its ears and sniffed the air. It got the smell of the tiger. It was alarmed so it whined and stood up. A black goat that was tied to a stake thirty feet down the street from the dog got the tigers scent. It stood up bleating.

The dog sniffed the air several times and barked at the alley in which the tiger stood. It barked again and darted into an alley on its side of the street. It stopped, turned around and peered out of the alley sniffing the air. The tigers scent was strong so it barked half a dozen times and scampered to the end of the alley.

T20 stepped onto the dirt road. He walked up the road in the opposite direction to where the dog had scampered off. He could hear the mongrel's barks from behind the mud huts. T20 sauntered along the road and noticed a doorless opening to a mud hut. He stopped and looked at it. The opening was covered with a couple of gunny sacks sewn together. T20 silently and nosily pushed his head between the gunny sack and peered in. Despite the darkness, he could make out the form of three sleeping figures. One was a male and two were females. The male was a Tendu leaf collector and the females were his wives.

T20 sniffed at the huts inner walls and slunk in crouched low. The humans were sleeping in the far corner of the hut. The tiger took his time and paw after slow paw he slunk towards his target. He hadn't noticed a child sleeping on the floor two feet away from his parent's feet. His fore paw stepped on the child who immediately woke up. The child felt something heavy on his abdomen so suddenly started bawling. T20 was startled by the sudden burst of noise directly under his face causing him to spring back.

"Mummy," the child wailed. "Mummy, something heavy was standing on my stomach. Yaaaaaaaaaa."

T20 realized it was a human he had stepped on. He was about to pounce on the child when the woman sat up. "Yes, what is it? Why are you crying?" she asked.

"Mummy something heavy squeezed my stomach."

The woman groped around the straw bed she and her family were sleeping on and made contact with her flashlight. She switched on the torch and saw the tiger. She screamed causing the husband and the other woman to get up.

T20 was startled and confused by the bright light. He was on the verge of attacking the child when the room lit up. Crouched low, he stared at the light, snarled at the screaming woman and sprang. In one deft move he grabbed her throat in his mouth, shook his own head violently snapping the woman's neck bone. She immediately kicked in painful throes as she lost consciousness.

The other humans took advantage of the tigers attack and made good their escape. The male grabbed the child by the legs and ran towards the huts door followed closely by the woman. They ran out of the doorway, turned right, and ran down the road accompanied by two terrified Pi dogs. The humans yelled as they ran accompanied with the dogs barks. They were too scared to look back and see if the tiger was chasing them. The male ran to his right and turned into an alley while the terrified female turned left in the opposite direction.

T20 held on to the gurgling writhing woman's throat and gave a couple of violent jerks with his head. The woman's gurgling stopped as her throes became week. Satisfied that he had put her out of action, he let go of her neck thereby allowing the upper part of the dead body to fall on the straw bed. He walked over to where the feet were, took a foot into his mouth and dragged the woman out of the hut into the open street. He let go of the leg, walked back to the neck, took a proper grip of it in his mouth, and headed into the jungle.

T20 had made a kill.

Chapter(13) The last fight

The old Ford Jeep roared down the rutted jungle road on the way to the village in which the tiger had killed and carried away the woman. Henry was as usual sitting on the passenger seat holding his rifle whose butt rested on the vehicles floorboard. Ram Singh was driving the vehicle and today he was driving it as though he was in a haste to reach the village. The villagers had tracked the kill and found the woman's remains in some bushes near a pile of rocks. The forest department officials had requested the dead ladies husband not to remove the remains as there were chances of the tiger coming back to the kill. The husband had turned down the request saying it was unholy leaving the mangled remains of his dead wife purposely so that the tiger would come back to eat it. "It is the husband's job to protect his wife. He takes the vows during his marriage to her," he said. "And if she dies, the least he can do is to cremate her with respect. Only a low down rascal will leave her mangled remains in bushes with flies buzzing over her and all sorts of scavengers gnawing into her decomposed body. Nothing doing, god was unkind to me and to her. I am taking the dead body away for cremation."

So it was decided that Henry would once more sit over a goat. Henry was tired now. He had been in Bhim Bandh for the last two months. He wanted to go back home, eat home food, and relax near his fish farm with his wife. He hadn't seen her for two months and felt it was improper of him to leave his wife, who was old now, for such a long period of time. "Today is the last day I'll sit over a kill." he said. "I will leave for PUSA tonight. If T20 comes back to the kill, which I doubt it will, and I manage to kill it, then well and good. But if I don't, you'll have to employ another hunter. My age doesn't allow me to go wondering into the jungle tracking a man eater who refuses to come back to its kill."

Ram Singh was worried. He was irritated. That is why he was driving the old vehicle at a speed he shouldn't be driving. "Sir," he said. "This is not the age of hunting tigers. Tigers are being preserved. The only hunters skilled today to hunt them are the poachers. Now where will I find a man who will hunt a man eating tiger?"

Henry looked at Ram Singh. "Morally it wouldn't be correct to kill the tiger," he said. "But it has killed over sixty people in a span of six months. That's quite a record. The people living in this area want it killed. The Indian Government should invite hunters and conservationists from outside, like the US or the UK. They could use dart guns to drug the animal and capture it. The forest department does not have a helicopter with which to spot the animal from the air. All the Indian Government has given the forest department in Jamui is a few ancient World war two vintage British army rifles and this ancient Jeep. So we don't have an option other than to shoot the animal. T20 is a beautiful animal. It is a pity it will have to be shot."

The Jeep roared on as it meandered through the forest. Ram Singh was worried. "Sir, are you sure you are going today?" he asked.

Henry shook and did a jig as the Jeep jerked as it skipped and hopped over obstacles. "Ram Singh, accept it. I have grown old. I cannot exert myself. I need a rest. I may or may not come back after a month. I'm not sure. I have a responsibility to my wife. We have lived together all our lives helping each other. She is elderly now. I haven't seen her for the last two months. This is criminal injustice to her from my side. She needs me. I have to be with her. Ram Singh, you will have to excuse me and make some other arrangement. I accept I have failed."

Ram Singh nodded his head and continued driving. The Jeep approached a tractor. He parped his horns at the slow moving vehicle, and when it made way, he overtook the vehicle and drove on with the Jeeps rear wheels kicking up dust at the tractor.

"But sir, what am I to do?" Ram Singh said. "Other than you, the only skilled hunters I can think of are the poachers."

Henry looked at Ram Singh. "Can I give you an illegal advice?" he asked.

Ram Singh nodded his head as he concentrated on the dirt track ahead of him. "Go ahead," he said.

The Jeep roared on as it meandered through the forest. Henry looked ahead at the rutted road. Ram Singh was driving too fast for his liking. "Get in touch with some poachers and put a reward on T20's head. Not dead, but alive. It will take time, but the poachers will be able to capture it. They are experts in this business."

Ram Singh shook his head as he steered the Jeep to the right as he negotiated a curve on the road. "That's not possible. They are criminals. Give the poachers ten rupee's and they'll demand fifty more. Tell them to kill T20 and they will kill the whole tiger population saying they mistook the tigers for T20. My job, which I inherited from people like you, is to keep them out of the forest. Not to invite them in."

Henry shrugged. "Have it your way," he said. "I was only suggesting."

Ram Singh smiled. "If I invite poachers to capture T20, do you know what the rascals will do? I will first have to allow them free and unhindered movement in the jungle. They will demand the prize money saying they were unable to capture the tiger. They will kill other tigers and claim that circumstances forced them to kill the tiger in self defense or they would have been killed themselves. They will say the felt is of no use to us. They will bribe some of my fellow forest officers and sell the felt in the market for an exorbitant amount. The bones and body parts will be smuggled to Hong Kong. The poachers will make triple profit than what they usually did."

Henry nodded his head in agreement. The Jeep had slowed down. They were approaching the section of road that was directly above the village. After driving for two minutes, Ram Singh slowed the vehicle down and stopped. He switched off the ignition and climbed down the vehicle while Henry climbed down the other side. The two walked to the edge of the road and looked down. The village was directly below them so the two entered a path and walked down the forested hill side.

Henry admired the scenic beauty around him as he trudged down behind Ram Singh. "The villagers in these villages may be leading a primitive life of penury, but they live in a paradise," Henry said. "If I hadn't inherited my fish ponds in PUSA, settling down here was not a bad option."

"You like Bhim Bandh?" Ram Singh asked as he brushed some ferns away.

"Lived here for quite a few years," Henry said. "I was the one who nurtured this forest. This is my baby."

"I know sir. You have become a part of Bhim Bandh folk lore. You were a very strict officer and did not allow wood cutters to cut wood."

The two approached a forest stream. They walked out of forest cover and were delighted to see a shoal of fishes dart in different directions. Water boatmen swam away while a kingfisher, which was hovering just ten feet above the water, got disturbed. It shrilled a shrill 'chiree-chiree' at the human intruders and flew away.

"This is the beauty of living in a forest," Henry said as he waded through the stream abreast to Ram Singh. "One doesn't have to earn money to live here. There is plenty of free food available. Simply catch a fish or a jungle fowl and eat it."

"Yes sir," Ram Singh said as he waded out of the stream and turned left. The village was now directly in front of them.

The two walked on silently. Henry was panting with the effort. They approached the village entrance and entered the village. They walked into the narrow alley that was the village's main street. They walked on and reached the village square where the villagers sat huddled together under a Banyan tree. Some villagers had gone with the dead body to the river side to cremate it.

Henry and Ram Singh approached the little group of people. Two baton holding khaki dressed forests guards were sitting cross legged with the villagers. On seeing Henry and Ram Singh approach, they stood up and said a Namaste to the two. The wood cutter who had escaped the tiger yesterday was sitting cross legged on the ground with the villagers. He also stood up in respect to the new comers.

Henry turned to Ram Singh and a forest guard and asked. "Who will lead us to the spot the dead body was found?"

Ram Singh pointed to the forest guard. "He will take us there. He knows this forest well and will take us to where they found the body."

"Then tell him to borrow a goat or a cow or a calf for today," Henry said.

Ram Singh turned to the forest guard and told him what Henry wanted. The guard at once turned to the villagers and asked them for a calf or a goat. A bare backed villager got up and led the forest guard away towards his hut.

"And tell him if the tiger kills the calf, the forest department will pay for it," Henry shouted at the receding figures.

The two waited for ten minutes and saw the forest guard emerge from an alley leading a brown colored calf by its tether. The owner of the calf trailed behind the animal. The forest guard walked up to Henry and looked at him for further orders.

"Lead the way," Henry said.

The forest guard walked down the village's single street followed by the second baton holding guard. Henry trailed behind the guard with Ram Singh bringing up the rear. The little group entered the forest and left the village behind. They followed a narrow path that ran through the forest. They walked for a kilometer along this path. This wasn't the route the tiger had taken. The forest guard had tracked the kill in the morning. They were taking Henry directly to the site where they found the dead body.

The forest guard reached a Sal tree, left the path and entered the jungles thick undergrowth. He pushed aside thick foliage to allow himself and the others through. They pushed through the foliage using the forest guard's batons to push aside the greenery as the guard pulled the calf along. They walked a hundred meters into the jungle pushing and shoving their way through the foliage when they entered a grassy opening. Directly in front of them in the far side of the grassy opening was a pile of huge rocks piled on top of each other. Ten feet above the ground, there was a narrow platform behind which the rocks were piled higher with the tip of the highest rock ten feet above the platform. Henry decided that the rocky platform was a good enough spot to sit over the bait.

"Tie the calf to those bushes," Henry pointed to the middle of open land where there was a thick tuft of magnolia bushes. "The calf can graze on the bushes while we wait up there."

"Where will we sit?" Ram Singh asked.

"On that platform on those rocks," Henry said as he shrugged his shoulder in surprise. Ram Singh was a forest officer and he was on the job for quite some years. But he was behaving like a rookie. He did not know head or tail about hunting.

The forest guard who was holding the calf's tether led the animal to the middle of the opening. He tied the tether to the base of the bushes and walked back. Henry was walking towards the pile of rocks with Ram Singh following him. He reached the base of the pile of rocks, slung his rifle to his shoulder and grappled up the rock face. Ram Singh followed him up with much difficulty. There were plenty of cracks and grooves on the rock face for Henry and Ram Singh to get a proper footing and a proper grip to climb up. Henry reached the top. Actually, his head looked over the rocky platform. It wasn't as comfortable as it looked from a distance with moss and tiny shrubs growing in little clumps. But it would do. Henry put his palms flat on the platform and hauled his heavy body up. He was soon standing on the platform. He looked down at Ram Singh and realized the latter needed help so he came down on his knees and extended his hand to Ram Singh. "Here hold my hand." Henry said.

Ram Singh grabbed Henry's hand and clasped it tightly in his own. Henry pulled up his hand and hauled the forest officer up.

"Thank you sir," Ram Singh said. "That was very kind of you."

"Forget the formalities," Henry replied as he made a sign to the forest guards who were standing on the ground below him to go. "The two of you go back to the village. If you hear anything unusual, like a shot from my rifle, gather a dozen men, make a big group, and come here."

The forest guards turned around and walked back the way they had come. They soon disappeared into the forest leaving Ram Singh and Henry alone to keep a vigil over the calf.

The two settled down made themselves as comfortable as was possible. Henry took out a white handkerchief from his trouser pocket and dusted the rocky ground with it. He laid the handkerchief neatly on the rock, sat down on it resting his back on the rock behind him. The rock towered ten feet above him. Ram Singh did the same and waited while he sat beside Henry.

"Today is my last day of sitting over a kill," Henry said. "No more hunting for me after this."

Ram Singh simply stared at the ground ahead of him. The two silently sat for two hours saying nothing.

"As usual I am feeling sleepy." Henry whispered.

"Please don't sleep sir," Ram Singh whispered back. "Not now."

The two humans sitting over the bait couldn't see into the future so, did not know that today was their lucky day. After sixty human kills, T20 went against his habit of not returning to his kill and inexplicably decided to return to the kill and check if it was where he had left it or the humans had taken it away. He was strolling silently through the jungle keeping himself hidden in the foliage so that jungle creatures did not see him and cry out an alarm to the forest.

It was one in the afternoon with a bright sun overhead. T20 reached a stream, crouched on his fore paws and lapped up water. After slaking his thirst, he waded into the stream and waded to the other side where he stood for a minute and looked around. A monkey saw him and made a din chattering with all its might telling the forest about the tiger. So T20 slunk into the bushes on the banks of the stream. He had slaked his thirst and was feeling hungry again. He would go and check if the humans had taken away his kill or it was still where he had left it in some bushes. If it was there he would gouge into it.

T20 strode up the hill concealing himself as much as possible. He brushed through ferns and branches and realized he was reaching the spot where he had left the kill. He was surprised when he reached the edge of the jungle adjacent to the clearing. He could hear an animal grazing. So he stopped and peered through the ferns at the open area in front of him. It was the place he had left the kill in. The tiger got a surprise. A calf was blissfully grazing on the grass. It was six months since he had eaten such an animal. Six months of eating human flesh. He felt that his mouth had healed and he could attempt to kill and eat the calf. It would be a nice change. He decided to go for the calf and kill it.

He waited for ten long minutes watching the calf. He studied the area behind it for anything dangerous. There was a pile of rocks in the far end of the clearing. He scanned the rocks for anything suspicious, and not seeing anything out of the way, he let his gaze shift back to the grazing animal. The animal looked delicious as T20 stared greedily at it. The wind turned and was now in the animals favor so the calf got the tigers scent. It stopped grazing, sniffed the air a couple of times, and turned its head around towards where T20 was hiding. It belched, pulled at its tether, belched again, and looked up at the rocks where the two humans were sitting. The two were not to be seen.

T20 was within fifteen meters of the calf. Realizing that his scent had alerted the calf, he decided to attack. It was now. He launched himself out of the ferns with a mighty roar and loped towards the calf. In five seconds he had reached and pounced on the calf grabbing its neck in his jaw and slamming the calf flat on the ground on its side. The stricken calf gurgled, found its voice and belched, lost its voice and gurgled again, belched and kicked with its legs as the tiger pinned it to the ground.

Up on the rocks, Henry and Ram Singh saw the attack. Henry's hands brought the rifle up with the butt against his shoulder as he leveled the barrel in line with the tiger that was grappling with the desperate calf.

"Shoot it sir," Ram Singh whispered.

Henry steadied the rifle and peered down its sights at the tiger and got a surprise. The tiger roared in his direction. And inexplicably let go of the stricken calf which at once stood up blocking Henry's view of the tiger. Henry saw the tiger lope into the jungle and disappear in the foliage. Henry shifted the barrel to align with the spot where the tiger had disappeared into the jungle. He swung the barrel slightly to the right and to the left scanning the jungle through the weapons sites. The tiger was nowhere to be seen so he lowered his rifle and scanned the area near the belching calf which was kicking and bucking around and pulling at its tether. The calf was a sorry sight.

"I feel like vomiting sir," Ram Singh whispered.

Henry was irritated. "Ram Singh I am ashamed of you," he whispered back. "Not now, if you vomit, I promise you I'll shove this barrel up your ass."

Ram Singh realized Henry was serious. He never used such language on him so he somehow controlled his stomach and with held his vomit as he peered into the forest to see if he could see anything.

"I wonder why it left the calf and loped into the forest," Henry wondered loudly. He did not know that while T20 was grappling the calf's neck it noticed a glint of bright light on the rock platform on which he and Ram Singh sat. The glint was sunlight bouncing off Henry's rifle barrel. T20 recognized the rifle and saw the human peering down it at him. It had experienced such a barrel before, especially the one that blew off his canine teeth. The tiger instantly let go of the calf and loped off into the jungle where it stopped, turned around, and watched the humans peering at the spot they had last seen him.

So there were humans on the rock. It meant that they wanted a fight and T20 was game. Humans were easier to kill than cows and calf's. His experience with the calf told him that his mouth hadn't healed fully yet. When he grabbed the calf's neck and applied pressure on his jaws, his mouth hurt. The pain was excruciating. This wasn't so with human hide. Their hide wasn't tough and was easy to bite through. If he could get the humans on the rocky platform, they would be easier to eat than the calf.

T20 decided to go for the humans and kill one. He slunk to his right and crept deeper into the jungle. He stretched his body low and advanced in slow motion. He took silent strides as he zig zagged through the foliage making sure he remained under cover. He skirted the patch of open land and continued his stalking of the humans till he was behind the pile of rocks on which the humans were sitting. He looked up and soundlessly started his slow climb up the rocks. He cautiously and silently climbed from rock to rock making no sound at all. He took his time going up slowly, making sure no stone or pebble rolled down. He climbed cautiously and rock after rock went below him as he went higher till he finally reached the top. He crouched low and peered down the other side. He saw the two human heads as they gazed at the bucking calf and the jungle beyond. T20 forgot that the mid day son was directly above him so he did not realize his shadow had fallen on Henry.

Henry was gazing at the farthest end of the clearing when he noticed the shadow envelope him. He realized the hunter was the hunted as he desperately without thinking swiveled around with his bottom acting as a fulcrum as he brought his rifle up pointing the barrel in the direction of the tiger. His swift reflex surprised the tiger which sprang. "Ram Singh jump," Henry yelled as he fired looking up at the springing tiger as he simultaneously kicked at the rock in front of him throwing himself backwards off the platform. He saw his bullet hit the animal's neck before he himself fell.

Ram Singh was fast. He did not jump. He simply dived off the rock and fell with a loud splat on his stomach next to Henry who fell on his back and rolled away. The tiger fell with a loud thud right on the spot where Henry had fallen. It stood up and roared next to a terrified Ram Singh's ears and loped into the jungle.

Henry was lying flat on the ground as he reloaded his rifle, sprang up on his knees and fired randomly at the escaping animal which loped into the forest. Loud crashing noises followed the animal as it loped away.

Henry pulled back the rifle bolt allowing the spent shell to hop out. He slammed back the bolt reloading the barrel as he stood up. He looked down at Ram Singh. The latter moaned as he held his left shoulder with his right hand. "Sir, I think I have dislocated my shoulder bone," he said as he stood up still holding his shoulder in his hand. "My leg hurts. I think I have broken some bones."

"Then you stay here while I go for the tiger. I saw the bullet hit the neck. I hit it. It is an injured tiger now. And the neck hit won't let it go far. I am going after it."

"I am coming with you," Ram Singh said. "I don't want to sit in the jungle all alone without a gun with an injured man eating tiger on the prowl. I will be safer behind you and your gun."

"Okay, then follow me. But remember it will be dangerous. You are not to panic."

Henry walked into the jungle in the direction where the tiger had disappeared. There were blood spots on the ground at various intervals. The tiger was bleeding so Henry followed the displaced foliage which showed the route the tiger had taken.

There was a sudden burst of noise in the jungle so the two stopped on their tracks. Birds had taken to the air and were flying all over the sky. They cried in loud squeals and squawks and chirps making a huge din over and across the jungle canopy. Their cries were accompanied by the excited chatter of a host of monkeys with peacocks shouting 'Kwa-aa-kwa-aa,' to everyone in general. The bird's cries were picked up by the shrill calls of chital deer and somewhere in the forest a sambar belched. The din was immense.

"The birds and jungle creatures have seen the tiger. That is why they are making a commotion. The din they are making means the tiger is in the open. It isn't hidden. Let us continue," Henry said.

The humans followed the blood spots and the displaced foliage for three hundred feet till they were confronted by an open patch of grassy land. At the far end were some bushes with the tiger lying on them. It seemed to have collapsed and was breathing heavily. A swarm of noisy birds were flying in circles above the fallen tiger with two dozen excited monkeys chattering wildly in nearby trees.

The wind was in the tigers favor so T20 got the humans scent. It lifted its head and saw the hunter lift the rifle and aim it at him. He had collapsed because the neck shot had smashed through some veins causing internal damage. But the anger of being hunted gave him the strength to stand up, crouch and roar, and launch himself forward in a charge. He bounded across the open land darting occasionally to the left and to the right as he ran towards the hunter.

Henry stood his ground peering down his rifle sight at the tiger as it charged. He fired as birds screamed in the sky. He missed the darting tiger but coolly peered down the rifle sight as the tiger continued darting to the left then to the right trying to dodge his line of fire as it ran. He pulled back the bolt allowing the spent shell to hop out and a fresh bullet to hop into the breach. He slammed back the bolt, and allowed the barrel to follow the darting tiger which was rapidly closing in. He fired and this time the bullet hit the tiger squarely on the head. The bullet smashed through the brains bringing the bounding tiger crashing to the ground. The animal roared in senseless anger and kicked in death throes as it lay on its side. Henry reloaded the rifle and aimed it at the head. He fired a third shot and saw a part of the skull split open. The tiger fell silent.

Henry pulled back the rifle bolt allowing the spent shell to skip out and a fresh bullet to hop out of the magazine into the breach. He slammed the bolt back reloading the rifle. He stared for a couple of minutes as he stood in the open ignoring the din in the sky. He waited for any sign of life in the tiger. There was none so he looked behind for Ram Singh. The latter wasn't behind him.

Still with his eyes on the dead tiger, Henry walked back a few steps. Ram Singh was nowhere around. Henry glanced to the right where he saw some movement. Ram Singh was sitting perched on a branch half way up a Sal tree.

"Ram Singh," Henry yelled. "I am ashamed of you. What sort of a forest officer are you?"

"I am proud of you sir," Ram Singh yelled back from his perch on the tree. "You killed the dreaded man eating tiger of Bhim Bandh. Thank you sir."

Ram Singh's voice was lost in the din the birds were making. They were celebrating the tiger's death. Henry stood there and looked at his dead child. A child he had nursed and lovingly watched as it grew into a strong and sturdy tiger making the forest of Bhim Bandh proud. It was his child whom he was forced to kill just because some city brats couldn't use their gun responsibly. He looked up sadly at the sky. The birds and all the living beings of the jungle were rejoicing at the child's death, at the king's death. They were informing the jungle of the kill.

The dreaded man eating tiger of Bhim Bandh was dead.

The End

Thank you for reading this novel. I hope you enjoyed it. I am a new author and it is important for me to get feedback on this book. So I humbly request you to leave a review. If you enjoyed this novel please forward it to your friends and relatives. This will give me strength to write more such stories. Thanking you.

And yes. The author's favorite book is "Killer Snake." Read it, you will enjoy it.

James Corbett.

"